ISBN-13: 978-0-913589-68-7
ISBN-10: 0-913589-68-3

Published by Williamson Books
An imprint of Ideals Publications
A Guideposts Company
Nashville, Tennessee
www.idealsbooks.com

Printed and bound in the United States of America

Library of Congress Cataloging-in-Publication Data

Carlson, Laurie M., 1952 -
    EcoArt! : earth-friendly art & crafts experiences for 3- to 9-year-
olds / Laurie Carlson; illustrated by Loretta Trezzo Braren.
            p. cm.
    "A Williamson kids can! book."
    Includes index.
    Summary: Presents art and craft projects that benefit the
environment through such activities as recycling.

    [1. Handicraft - Juvenile literature. 2. Nature craft - Juvenile
literature. 3. Recycling (Waste, etc.) - Juvenile literature. (1.
Handicraft. 2. Nature Craft. 3. Recycling (Waste)]
    I. Braren, Loretta Trezzo, ill. II. Title.
    TT160.C35 1992   92-21347
745.5 - dc20   CIP
                                                     AC

Kids Can!® Series Editor: Susan Williamson
Cover design by: Trezzo-Braren Studio
Illustrations by: Loretta Trezzo Braren
Project diagrams by: Laurie Carlson

Kids Can!® is a registered trademark of Ideals Publications.

20 19 18 17

Laurie Carlson is also the author of Williamson Books'
Kids Create! Art & Craft Experiences for 3- to 9-Year-Olds.

For my parents

I would like to thank all the children who have shared their ideas and enthusiasm with me, and the many environmental groups that are working for all of us. Thanks as well to the staff at Williamson Publishing for helping me create books out of dreams.

Earth-Friendly Art & Craft Experiences
♥ for 3- to 9-year-olds ♥

Laurie Carlson

♥

Illustrated by Loretta Trezzo Braren

Nashville, Tennessee

"Every genuine work of art has as much reason for being as the earth and the sun."

Ralph Waldo Emerson

ART SPEAK

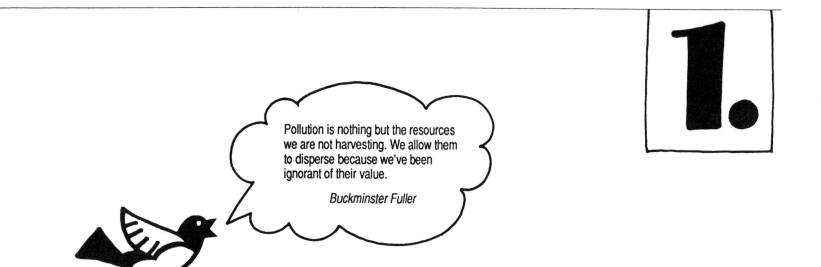

Pollution is nothing but the resources we are not harvesting. We allow them to disperse because we've been ignorant of their value.

Buckminster Fuller

1.

TAKE CHARGE!

Use it up,
Wear it out,
Make it do,
Or do without!

That wise, old saying was probably around when your grandparents and great-grandparents were the same age as you are now! In those days, people made a great effort to be frugal which means they took care of their few possessions and made them last, and last, and last. Everyone — rich or poor, young or old — took pride in not wasting anything, and reusing clothes and tools was a way of life. "Buying new" was done carefully and thoughtfully, and more often than not, families made what they needed, or did without.

Well, for many of us, all that has changed now. People tend to buy whatever they can afford, and as we all know, throw a lot of "stuff" out, only to go to the store and buy something else "brand new." But where do all of the materials come from to make toys, and gadgets, and stationery, and packaged frozen foods? And where does all the energy come from to run the factories and power the trucks that carry these things to the stores? And what happens to all the trees and wildlife that must be removed to build shopping centers and malls for the stores that sell these things? And what happens to our forests, and plants, and animals, and fresh water, and fresh air in the process?

You already know the answer to that, don't you! Many of us around the world are using up our natural resources at a very, very fast rate, and along the way we are creating big problems — endangered species like the giant panda, quickly disappearing forests like the tropical rain forests, dirty air and water that aren't fit to breathe and drink, and overflowing landfills because we have so much garbage!

You can make a difference!

Even though it sounds pretty bleak, and you may wonder what is to become of our wonderful earth, there is some really good news! You can make a difference! You and I, and our friends, and our family — can make a difference that will count and will help the earth. We're the ones who will do it. We will set up a home recycling center (see page 148), we'll keep a rag bag (see page 154) and an art inspiration box (see page 145). We'll learn to treat nature's wonders with respect and care (see page 89). We'll avoid products that are over-packaged, and always choose to buy things that aren't made with styrofoam or other materials that will clog our landfills.

Best of all, we will learn to make things just like people did years ago, and in the process we will discover just how creative and imaginative we can be. We can make our own paper, pastes, and dyes (see pages 13 to 30). And then, we can make everything from vases to sculptures, to games and dolls, to castles and jewelry, to cornhusk wreaths and bird feeders. *We don't need brand new; homemade is better — especially when we are reusing and recycling!*

Let's get specific

Things won't change overnight. It will take some thinking about what we do every day. If we think about the choices we make, then we can leave the world even better than we found it. Attitude is everything, so don't feel that you are sacrificing enjoyment by being more environmentally aware. Change must come through consuming less, reusing and recycling, and shopping smart. Kids like you will become the teachers to the grown-ups who have never had to recycle or reuse before now. As you ask your parents and grandparents to please recycle, and as you set a good example for your younger sisters and brothers, we will all learn to be better citizens of the earth, together. You will make a difference!

The best way to save the earth is to just not use up so much of it. You and I have to stop buying useless things that we really don't want or need. Shop for things that will last and can be repaired or refilled, instead of being disposable. People have always reused things in order to save money. Now we have to think about reusing things in order to save the open spaces, forests, and water.

Practice *precycling* by looking at items from an environmental viewpoint — *before* buying them. Select the items that have less packaging,

use up less of the environment, and have lasting value.

Many things can be *recycled*, using the materials from existing products to create new ones. Newspapers can be recycled into new paper. Aluminum cans, glass, and some plastics can be brought to recycling centers where they will be used to make new aluminum cans, glass jars and bottles, and some plastic containers, thereby saving natural resources and energy.

Reusing means getting as much wear and tear out of every item you have for as long as possible, and then thinking up new uses for the old parts. All of us can reuse materials in our everyday lives, and we never have to leave our houses or use any additional natural resources. There are lots of fun and interesting items you can make from things that would usually go in the garbage. Start an art inspiration box right now, for things you can save. It will provide a ready source of supplies when you are working on projects.

What is EcoArt?

My guess is that you can already figure out what EcoArt is, because you already understand so much about our earth. *Ecology*, as you know, is the study of how plants and animals and people interact with their environment. A lot of scientists are concerned about the *balance of nature* which is the idea that nature, when left to its own, will take care of itself, but when humankind starts polluting the air and water, for example, the balance is thrown off and some creatures begin to die while others become too plentiful.

So what does this have to do with art? Well, that is a good question. All of the art and craft projects in this book relate to good ecological practices — respect for nature and a love of nature, good recycling efforts, and reusing everything that you possibly can. As you look to nature for inspiration, you will be strengthening your commitment to do your part to save the earth. As you create treasures out of trash, you will open your eyes to all sorts of possibilities for using things that would otherwise end up in our landfills. There really is an art to safeguarding our ecology — in more ways than one!

The projects in this book will help you look at the world around you with different eyes. Begin noticing

the tiny signs of life around you: plants, insects, birds, shells, the variety of leaves, and bark, and flower petals. Be alert to your surroundings, listening to bird calls, watching a daddy long legs gracefully and silently walk across some pebbles, and smelling the fragrance in weeds. Begin to look at nature's bounty — nuts, weeds, pods, moss, twigs, shells — as gifts to you that you can make

into wonderful decorative and useful items. Watch for things to renew and reuse: paper products, discarded toys, empty boxes. As you begin to create with natural and reusable materials, you will begin to respect and appreciate everything around you more. Go ahead — with wonder, and questions, and imagination — and have a great time!

SAFETY FIRST!

To ensure your safety and well-being, please observe these safety measures. They really are important.

Paraffin: Wax and paraffin should be melted in a can placed in the top of a double boiler (water in both parts of double boiler). *A grown-up must always do this part of a project. Paraffin is flammable.*

Hot glue gun: These are very handy, but must be used by grown-ups. If a grown-up isn't around, use a tacky-type glue instead, and press very hard until glue holds.

Balloons: Balloons may seem safe to play and create with, and they are, but they can be very dangerous for little children who still put things in their mouths. Be sure to pick up any pieces of popped balloons and deflated balloons so that little children won't pick them up. Thank you.

Craft knives: Grown-ups should use the craft knives and sharp scissors. Ask them to show you correct methods for safe use and handling.

Ventilation: Proper ventilation is necessary when using rubber cement and many fixatives. Acrylic sprays are extremely flammable as well as toxic. (Non-aerosol hair spray is a good substitute.) Grown-ups should apply fixatives, not children.

Wild plants: Wild plants are beautiful to look at and to collect, but never eat them. As you know, many of them are poisonous.

Thank you for being so careful.

Be a recycling sleuth! You can tell if paper is made from recycled paper by the tiny flecks of fiber showing in it. Recycled cardboard is gray, like the inside of cereal boxes.

• A NOTE TO PARENTS, TEACHERS, & CARE-GIVERS •

Today's child is in danger of losing touch with nature. The natural world is far from our apartments and lifestyles. For many, the natural play in woods, streams, mud puddles, and snowbanks that past generations so enjoyed, is but an image from a picture book. Yet, children gravitate to anything in its natural state. They enjoy working with all kinds of natural materials: pine cones, pods and weeds, shells, moss, driftwood, smooth stones, wildflowers, feathers, and vines. They are intrigued by the feel of these items in their hands, by the process of collecting materials while feeling the wind in their hair, and by the earthy scent of the forest.

It is this natural world that our children are in danger of never experiencing and never appreciating; it is not found in stores, nor advertised on television. It does not draw attention to itself artificially. Sadly, what once was common, has now become unusual.

Given the opportunity, children from all walks of life respond to the excitement and warmth of the natural world. They quickly come to respect its wonder and its fragility. Every child becomes a nurturer when placed in a natural setting. Every child discovers an inner peace and hidden creativity when given the chance to interact with nature.

It is my hope that children using this book will awaken this creative impulse, will experience nature with all of their senses, and will treasure that experience, for it is only through a personal sense of awe that our children will make the monumental effort to put our earth first. I ask of you as parents, and teachers, and care-givers to encourage their efforts; let them awaken in you the energy and interest to share in their efforts to save their earth.

Toward a Positive Experience

Each project is identified as to the approximate degree of difficulty involved to confidently complete it. Look for the leaves to identify the suggested range of ability or dexterity each project might involve.

🍁 = Few fine motor skills needed. Adults may need to help very young children by preparing some of the materials ahead of time. With very little adult assistance, these projects should delight most children.

🍁🍁 = Skills such as cutting, folding, using a template, or painting may be required. Young children need practice with these skills, but adults should avoid creating frustrating experiences for those truly too young to handle them. Most children enjoy these projects and will want to experiment with the wider range of mediums and tools.

🍁🍁🍁 = More involved projects that require manual dexterity and a variety of steps to completion. Most children will do just fine with these, especially if they are left to improvise and use their own creative approaches.

These indicators of skill level are quite arbitrary. Don't let them limit your choice of project. If a project is interesting, fun, and appropriate, work around any part that seems beyond a child. Most projects have at least some part that all children can participate in. Collecting materials and thinking about new uses for old objects will tantalize even the youngest creator. Kids are extremely versatile, especially when they really want to do something. Usually they are very willing to stretch their abilities or find clever shortcuts.

Clock Watchers

Most projects in this book can be completed in twenty to thirty minutes, or less. Because time allowances are necessary for using some mediums and completing some of the projects, I've identified those projects requiring more than one hour to complete. Look for the little clock which is your signal that the project takes more than one hour. Read through these projects because many of them have convenient stopping points. If you can leave your materials out and come back later, the time may not be a factor.

In some cases, materials must be prepared ahead of time, or drying or baking time is required. This is not included in the estimate. Allow extra time for drying which varies with the medium used, as well as thickness of the project, humidity level, and temperature.

2

MAKING YOUR OWN
ART & CRAFT SUPPLIES

NATURAL ART

Nature provides many gifts. The brilliant colors of autumn leaves, the intricate symmetry of a bird's feather, the glistening beauty in a chunk of rock, the cracked patterns in mud as it dries — all nourish our creativity. Nature surrounds us with its beauty and strength. If we stop and look closely, we see that nature has given us inspiration for our own art. The musical trill of a bird call, the feel of a rabbit's downy coat, the patterns in clouds above us — everywhere is inspiration for our eyes, our ears, and our fingertips.

Artists, musicians, and poets have been inspired by nature in many ways. Let it inspire you, too. As you look for the perfect pebble for a project, or choose an interesting leaf or branch, you will be joining with nature to shape your creations.

Natural art can be found in the tiniest rock, the simplest shell. It inspires us and gives us encouragement. But natural art is fragile and can be easily lost. To find the twig, you must have a tree. To smell a wildflower, there must be meadows for them to bloom in. To watch a creature, there must be space and nourishment for it to survive. If we protect and preserve the natural world, the quiet path or cooling creek will always be there for us.

QUILL PEN

MATERIALS

Feather

Ink or tempera paint

Scissors or knife

You can make a pen like those used by writers from the sixth century until the mid-nineteenth century, when the steel pen point was invented.

Feathers from geese were most commonly used. Swan feathers were more expensive. Crow's feathers were best for creating fine lines.

In order to make your own quill pen, you need to find or purchase a feather. Look outside and see if you can find any feathers in your yard or along the beach. (Wash your hands after handling.) Chicken or turkey feathers are sold in most craft supply shops, if you can't find any.

With scissors or a sharp knife, snip off the end at a slant. Dip the cut end into ink or paint and write just like your ancestors might have!

When the tip wears down, snip it off a bit more, to create a fresh sharp tip. Now that is really recycling!

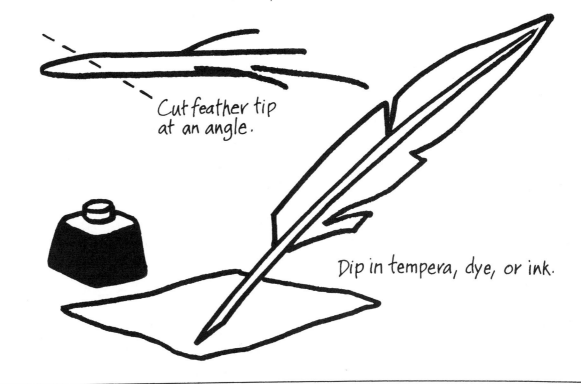

Cut feather tip at an angle.

Dip in tempera, dye, or ink.

Feathers are made of keratin, a fibrous protein that also makes up hair.

NATURE NOTE

NATURAL DYES ✻ ✻ ✻ ✻ ✻ ✻ ✻ ✻ ✻ ✻

MATERIALS

Plant materials

Cloth or paper to dye

Large pot and water

Wooden spoon

Creating dyes from natural plant materials is fun and interesting. Put on your old clothes and go gathering and collecting. You'll be so surprised to see what colors your gathered materials will produce. You can use your natural dyes to color cotton, or wool yarn, or fabrics. Use your dyes to paint on paper or fabric, to color cornhusks, feathers, straw, egg shells, and, of course, cotton T-shirts and socks. You can even use your natural dye to color eggs, or just pour the dye into jars and paint with water-color brushes.

The colors you can make are soft, natural, and sometimes muted. To get a stronger color, let items soak for a longer time or redye in freshly gathered materials.

Here's what to gather to make a variety of natural dyes:

For this color:	Use one of these materials:
Yellow	Goldenrod, sassafras flower, pomegranate rinds, onion skins, willow tree leaves, marigolds, orange peels
Red	Cherries, birch bark (gathered from the ground only)
Rose	Willow bark (gathered from the ground only)
Purple	Blackberries, elderberries
Blue	Red cabbage leaves, sunflower seeds
Green	Carrot tops, grass clippings, spinach, moss
Tan	Walnut shells, tea leaves, instant coffee

Yellow=Marigolds

Red=Cherries

Blue=Sunflower Seeds

Green=Carrot Tops

Tan=Tea Leaves

If you are unable to gather natural plant materials to make your dyes, you can purchase frozen or canned berries or vegetables to create the dye. To use canned beets, strain the liquid and add 2 teaspoons of vinegar. To use frozen blueberries or blackberries, let them thaw in a bowl and press out the juice.

Experiment with other flowers, berries, and leafy materials you find. Boil them in water to see what color they create. And guess what? Rusty nails can be added to a dye to make the color darker, so you can be cleaning up while gathering, too.

To prepare dyes from any of these natural materials, first cut or tear the plant materials in small pieces and place in a large pot. Add enough water to cover the material. Ask a grown-up to help you boil it for 5 – 20 minutes, until the water reaches the color intensity you want. With help, strain the mixture into a cut-down plastic jug through a piece of cheesecloth, or the foot section of a pair of panty hose. Add a tablespoon of vinegar to act as a *mordant* to the dye bath. The mordant will set, or keep, the color. Now, have a grown-up help you reheat the dye bath in a large saucepan.

Experiment by dipping fabric, yarn, or paper into the dye to check color. If you like the color, let the material

Tear the plant materials in small pieces & cover with water. Boil for 5 to 20 minutes.

you are dying simmer in the dye bath, until it reaches the color you like. Stir or turn it to be sure the color covers evenly.

When you like the color of the dyed material, rinse it in water. Keep rinsing in fresh water, until the rinse water is clear. Spread the material out and let dry.

If you want, you can freeze the dye water and use it again at a later time.

Be sure to avoid eating or drinking any of the plant materials or natural dyes because many wild plants, flowers, leaves, stems, and roots are poisonous.

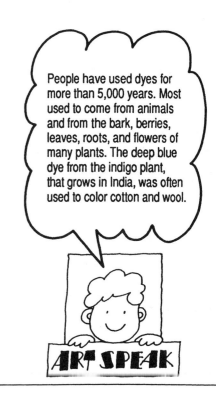

People have used dyes for more than 5,000 years. Most used to come from animals and from the bark, berries, leaves, roots, and flowers of many plants. The deep blue dye from the indigo plant, that grows in India, was often used to color cotton and wool.

ART SPEAK

HOMEMADE RECYCLED PAPER

MATTERIALS

Newspaper or other waste paper

Plant materials: flower petals, leaves, weeds, onion skins

Water

Dishpan

Screening, about 8" x 8"

Towels

Bucket

Pieces of old bedsheet material, about 12" x 12"

Sponge

Electric blender or mixer

The first U.S. paper mill was built in 1690. The paper was made from old cotton and linen rags. It was 200 years later when wood pulp from trees was used to make paper.

Paper has been made from a variety of natural materials such as cotton, mulberry bark, hemp, and grass. Today, it is usually made from pulp that is produced by grinding up trees. Because paper is so important to us, and because we use so much of it, we need to be careful not to waste it. Remember that it takes only seconds to use a paper tissue or napkin, but decades for a tree to grow.

Paper is one item that can be completely recycled. Old newspapers can be turned into wet pulp and pressed into fresh paper again and again. You can recycle paper by making your own handmade paper from scraps of waste paper.

1. Tear paper & soak in water.

2. Blend the soaked paper with water in a blender.

Tear the waste paper into small pieces, and soak it overnight in a bucket of water. Place a few handfuls of the soaked paper into a blender and fill it about half full with water. Blend in short bursts to break the material up. Add torn bits of leaves, flower petals, grass, weeds, or whatever. You can put in some natural dyes or food coloring, too.

Now lay the piece of screen in the dishpan, and then fill the dishpan with about 3" of water. Pour the pulp from the blender into the dishpan. Slide the piece of screen back and forth through the mixture, and then lift it straight up. The pulp will be distributed evenly on the screen. Lay the screen on a towel to drain.

Place a piece of old fabric or sheeting on top of the pulp, and press firmly with a sponge to remove the excess water. Continue until all water is removed from the pulp.

Turn the screen over, releasing the paper onto the sheeting material. Lay it on a flat surface to dry. Peel the paper away from the cloth when it is dry.

To hasten the drying process, lay a second sheet of fabric on top of the strained paper and ask a grown-up to press with a heated iron. This also makes the paper flatter and smoother in texture.

3. Pour pulp into a dishpan. Slide the screen, then lift up, trapping pulp on the screen.

4. Place as shown & sponge up excess water. Iron with steam iron if desired.

SPONGE

FABRIC SHEET

TOWEL

SCREEN WITH PULP

STEM PAINT BRUSH & CLAY PAINT �֍ ✳ ✳ ✳

MATERIALS ★★🕐

Soft plant stalk: yucca, iris or cattail stem, or cornhusk

Knife

Rock

Clay (freshly dug or bought)

White glue

Native Americans in the Southwest used to chew the ends of yucca stalks to soften them and then use the "brush" to paint pottery with delicate brush strokes.

To make your own stem paint brush, break or cut a plant stalk to get a piece 8" – 10" long. Break up the fibers at one end to make your brush's "bristles," by cutting them with a knife, shredding in narrow strips, or mashing the end with a rock. Work at it until the fibers are separated and brush-like. *Don't chew on plant materials, as they may be poisonous.*

Pound the end of the stem with a rock to create "bristles."

CLAY + WATER + WHITE GLUE = CLAY PAINT

Paint with your stem paint brush.

BROWN PAPER BAG

Great! Now you're ready to make some *clay paints* like the Native Americans did (or you can paint with poster paints). Begin looking for some soft clay in your backyard or in your neighborhood. Dig a bit here and there, squishing the clay with your fingers until you find some that sticks together. Depending upon where you live, natural clay can be chocolate brown, light tan, or orange-red.

After you have dug some clay, let it dry; then, pound or break it up into small pieces. Pick out any rocks, sticks, or roots.

Now, add some water and let it soak until the clay is dissolved. Stir and add a bit more water and a squirt of white glue, until the clay paint is smooth. Paint on heavy cardboard or brown paper bags. Crumple the bags, then smooth flat, and they will resemble animal hide.

NATURAL CLAY ✳ ✳ ✳ ✳ ✳ ✳ ✳ ✳ ✳ ✳ ✳

If you live in an area where soft, pliable clay is available for the digging, you'll have a great time digging, then shaping and sculpting items that can be dried in the sun. While sun-dried clay pieces aren't waterproof or permanent, if they are carefully stored, they can last for many, many years.

Locate clay that is fine textured, and free of leaves, gravel, and sticks. If you need to clean the clay, dilute it with water, and strain it through a sieve or colander to remove the debris. Let the diluted clay dry in the sun, until it is thick enough to work with. If you add a few tablespoons of white glue to the clay, it will dry harder.

To shape objects from clay, you will want to use a clump the size of your fist. To add arms, legs, or a neck, use your fingers to pull the clay into shape. (If you roll tiny pieces and add them to the clay body for arms and legs, they will often break off later.) Remember, pull the sculpture into shape from the larger ball. If you don't like the sculpture, just squish it all back into a ball and start again.

When working with clay, have a pan of water handy. Dip your fingertips in it to moisten and smooth the clay as you work it. Use sticks, stones, and tools such as nails or dull knives to trim and decorate your sculptures. You can press bits of twigs, feathers or leaves into the clay to add interesting details, since you will be air-drying your sculpture.

Try your hand at shaping simple clay animals, pots, napkin rings, or potpourri bowls.

Strain the clay to remove leaves, gravel, and sticks.

Pull the clay into shape.

MATERIALS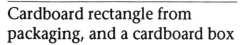

Cardboard rectangle from packaging, and a cardboard box

Clothespins

Serrated knife (grown-up use)

Yarn or string

If you want to take along additional art supplies for sketching or painting, make a simple easel from a box.

Cut away one side of the box as shown. Ask a grown-up to help, using a serrated knife to cut. Angle the cut slightly so the paper will be held at the appropriate angle. Place a larger rectangle of cardboard, or your clipboard, across the opening and clip your paper to it. Your supplies can be kept inside the box.

Make a clipboard for sketching or writing when you go on outdoor hikes. Find a rectangle of heavy cardboard (or get help cutting one from a grocery box). Paint or decorate the cardboard as you wish. You can glue on used gift wrap, paint with left-over latex housepaint, or cover with crayon rubbings over leaves. Fasten your paper to the clipboard with clothespins or heavy clips. To keep your pencil handy, punch a hole in a corner of the clipboard and tie a length of yarn or string from it to the end of your pencil.

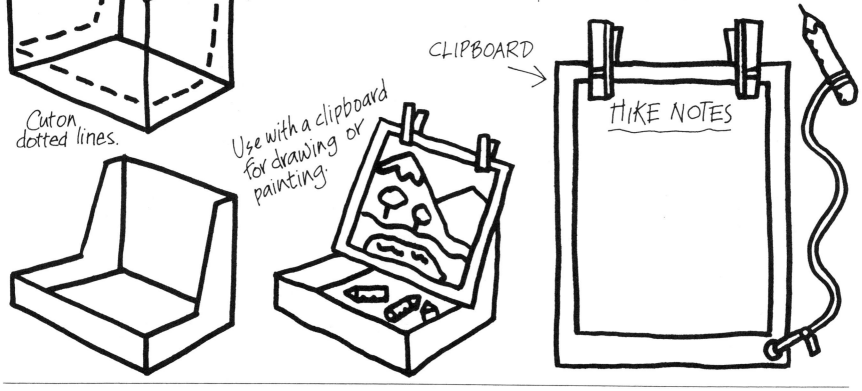

Cut on dotted lines.

Use with a clipboard for drawing or painting.

CLIPBOARD

HIKE NOTES

HOMEMADE SUPPLIES

Make your own! If you like to do art and craft projects, you know that the materials often cost a lot or are toxic or hazardous to your environment, if not used properly. To be safe and to save the earth (and some money), why not make some earth-friendly, natural art supplies?

Here are some "art and craft recipes" that you may want to try. Many can be stored for use in other projects throughout this book.

PASTES & GLUES ★ ★ ★ ★ ★ ★ ★ ★ ★ ★

Homemade pastes and glues are perfect for any project using paper or cardboard. The glues are best for projects needing small amounts of adhesive. They work with most papers, fabric scraps, and yarn. The pastes are best for paper projects, whether you are using brown bags, wallpaper scraps, or old newspapers. If you want to make collages or papier-mache, use the paste recipes, but stir in additional water until the mixture is the thickness of pancake batter. Whatever recipe you choose, it will begin to mold and sour in a few days, unless you refrigerate it or add a natural preservative, such as oil of cloves or oil of wintergreen.

Cornstarch Glue

MATERIALS

3 tablespoons cornstarch

4 tablespoons cold water

2 cups hot water

Saucepan and spoon

Ask a grown-up to help you use the stove. Mix the cornstarch and cold water in a saucepan. When smooth, begin pouring in the hot water, stirring as you add it. Heat the mixture to medium heat and cook until it begins to thicken. Stir it constantly. When it's thick, remove it from the heat and let cool. Pour into a clean dish detergent squeeze bottle or other type of container, label the bottle "glue," and store in the refrigerator when not using.

Flour and Water Paste

MATERIALS

1/2 cup flour

3/4 cup cold water

3 cups hot water

Saucepan and spoon

Ask a grown-up to help you use the stove. Put the flour and cold water into a saucepan, stirring to blend smooth. Add the hot water, stirring constantly. Heat and stir until mixture is thick and smooth. Let cool and pour into a squeeze-type container, like one from shampoo or mustard. Label the bottle "paste," and store in the refrigerator.

Library Paste

Makes a thick paste that spreads with your fingers. Use it on paper projects.

MATERIALS

1/2 cup sugar

1/2 cup flour

2 cups water

1/2 teaspoon alum
(from supermarket or drugstore)

Oil of cloves, optional
(from drugstore)

Saucepan and spoon

Ask a grown-up to help you at the stove. Mix everything (except oil) together in a saucepan, and heat to medium, stirring constantly. When the mixture thickens, remove from the heat and let it cool. If you want to keep this paste for up to several months, add 15 drops of oil of cloves to keep it from spoiling. Label and store in covered containers, like margarine or cottage cheese tubs.

Crazy Paste

My favorite! This paste uses unusual ingredients to make a smooth paste that dries without flaking or cracking. It dries clear, and works well with most craft materials.

MATERIALS

1/4 cup cornstarch

3/4 cup water

2 tablespoons corn syrup

1 teaspoon white vinegar

1/4 teaspoon oil of wintergreen, optional preservative

Medium saucepan and spoon

Ask a grown-up to help you at the stove. Mix the cornstarch and water in the saucepan. Add the corn syrup and vinegar. Stir and cook over medium heat until the mixture thickens. It will take a few minutes; then it will begin to thicken quickly. Continue stirring as it thickens. Remove from heat. To add a preservative, stir in 1/4 teaspoon of oil of wintergreen. This paste will get thicker as it cools. Label and keep in a covered container (like a cottage cheese container) for about two months. Without oil of wintergreen, store in the refrigerator for about two weeks.

Bookbinder's Paste

Here's an old recipe that professional bookbinders used long ago. It's simple, inexpensive, and uses no chemicals. It works for any type of paper-pasting project. It cleans up with water and the paper dries flat and smooth.

This recipe makes about five cups of paste which will be enough for several projects.

MATERIALS

1 cup flour

1 cup cold water

4 or 5 cups of very hot water

Saucepan and spoon

Put the flour in a saucepan and slowly stir in the cup of cold water. Stir till smooth, breaking up any lumps. Ask a grown-up to help you slowly pour in the hot water, a cup at a time. Place on medium heat. Cook for three minutes, stirring all the time. Let it cool; then it's ready to use. Use a sponge, paint brush, or your fingers to spread it.

This paste will keep for a few days, if covered and refrigerated. If you want to keep it longer, add 2 teaspoons of powdered alum or 3 drops of oil of cloves.

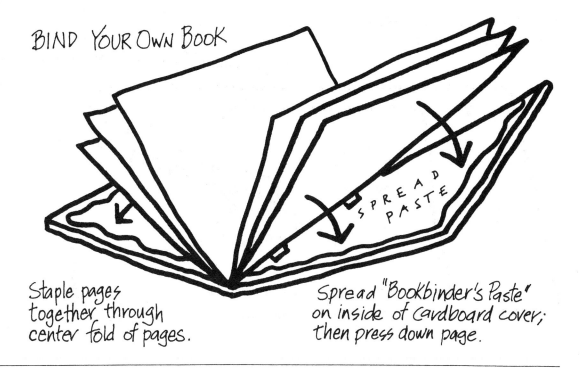

BIND YOUR OWN BOOK

SPREAD PASTE

Staple pages together through center fold of pages.

Spread "Bookbinder's Paste" on inside of cardboard cover; then press down page.

HOMEMADE FINGER PAINT ★ ★ ★ ★ ★ ★

Finger paints can be made from many things. You can use shaving cream to finger paint on washable surfaces. Liquid starch can be colored with powdered tempera or a squirt of food coloring. In the winter, mix a bit of Bon Ami and water in a jar lid and fingerpaint snowflake designs on windows. Wipe off with a wet cloth to clean up.

MATERIALS

1/2 cup flour

2 cups water

Food coloring

Paper: save used typing and copier paper; use the backside

Newspapers

Saucepan and spoon

Baby food jars, yogurt containers, or similar containers

Mix the flour with a little water, stirring out the lumps. When smooth, slowly stir in the rest of the water. Ask a grown-up to help you cook over medium heat, stirring constantly until the mixture gets thick and shiny.

Carefully pour some of the mixture into each jar. (You may want to make a funnel to do this. See how to do it on page 128.) Stir in drops of food coloring until the paint is bright and the color you want. Let cool.

While waiting, cover the table or floor painting area with old newspapers. Wet the painting paper with water, smoothing the wet paper out on the newspapers. Spoon the finger paint onto the paper and get started!

Salt can be sprinkled into the wet paint to create a sparkling effect when dry. Use this technique on dark-colored paper for snow scenes or eerie ghosts.

TOOLS ★ ★ ★ ★ ★

MATERIALS ✳

Old plastic bottles

Fine tip permanent marking pen

Scissors or craft knife

Nail or hole punch

YARN NEEDLES

Make some of your own art and craft tools, so you'll have them ready when you need them. You can make brushes (see page 20), remelt crayons (see page 30) and make paper (see page 18).

To make *templates* and *stencils*, cut flat areas from plastic bottles and packaging materials. Draw your design with a marking pen; then, cut it out with scissors or craft knife.

Make simple *yarn needles* for stitching, weaving, and stringing objects by cutting thin needle shapes from a plastic jug. Use a hole punch or nail to make a hole at one end. Thread with yarn or embroidery thread. Cut as many as you need, in several sizes.

HOMEMADE YARN ★

MATERIALS ✳✳

Old T-shirts

Scissors

Use your homemade yarn any time you need a heavy yarn or string — for wrapping packages, weaving, or creating toys and puppets. Remove any pockets, cuffs, or trim from the T-shirt, and cut away the hem and sleeves. Begin cutting at the bottom of the shirt, and cut an inch-wide strip in a continuous spiral around the shirt. When you stretch the yarn, the cut ends will curl under, giving it a tubular shape. Roll it in a ball and save for your projects. You can also obtain yarn for projects by unraveling old knitted scarves, sweaters, or whatever, and saving the yarn in balls.

WEAVING LOOMS & LOOPS ★ ★ ★ ★ ★ ★

★★★

Make the loom by tapping long nails into a board in the shape of a 12" square. Cut the loops about 1" wide from the leg section of old panty hose and colorful tights. Hook the ends of the loops on the nails. Weave loops over and under until the loom is full. To finish the ends, slip one loop end off the nail and through the next loop, until you come to the last loop. Make a slip knot with it and tuck the loop back inside the weaving.

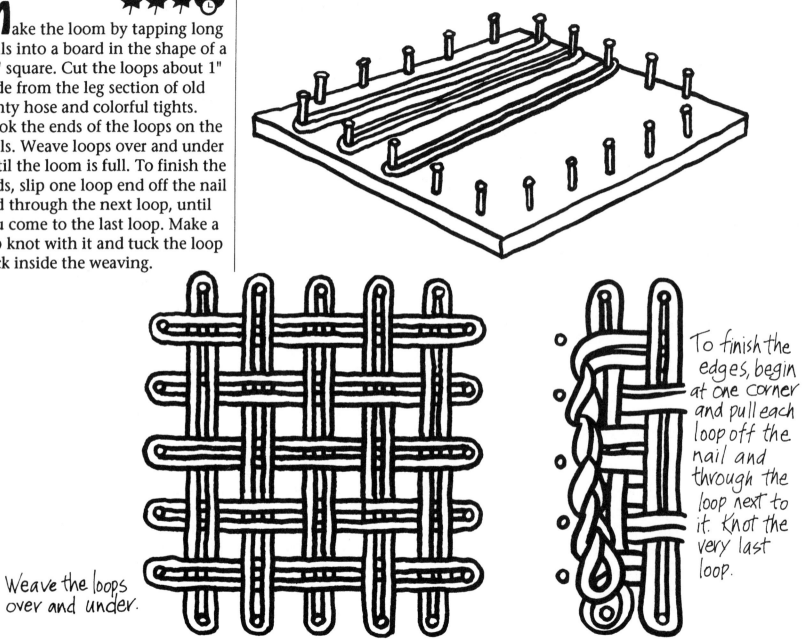

Weave the loops over and under.

To finish the edges, begin at one corner and pull each loop off the nail and through the loop next to it. Knot the very last loop.

CLAYS & DOUGHS ★ ★ ★ ★ ★ ★ ★ ★ ★

Creative Clay

This recipe makes a soft clay that can be cut with cookie cutters or shaped, and then air-dried until hard. It can be painted or decorated with acrylics, tempera, watercolors, or markers.

To give a shiny finish, coat with acrylic floor wax.

MATERIALS

1 cup cornstarch

1 cup baking soda

1 1/4 cups cold water

Saucepan and spoon

Ask a grown-up to help you mix ingredients together in a saucepan over medium heat, stirring constantly. Stir, about 5 minutes until it's very thick — like mashed potatoes. Cool on a plate until you can work with your hands. Roll, cut, or shape as you wish. Let dry for about 2 days. Paint or finish as you like.

If you are making ornaments, press a paper clip into the soft clay for a hanger, or punch holes with a nail before the clay dries.

Baker's Clay

This clay is best made fresh before each work session, because it doesn't keep well.

MATERIALS

4 cups flour

1 cup salt

1 1/2 cups warm water

Used aluminum foil

Bowl and spoon

Cookie sheet

Mix flour and salt in the bowl. Slowly add the water, stirring until it becomes stiff; then use your hands to knead the mixture. Knead thoroughly for at least 5 minutes on the table top, adding more flour as needed. Place the dough in a covered container or old plastic bag, taking out only small amounts at a time as you work.

This dough can be hand-formed into shapes, rolled flat to cut with cookie cutters, or pressed into candy and cookie molds. Avoid making thick projects, as the inside will not cook properly and the outside will crack. Instead, press the dough over crushed foil armatures to make large pieces, and then bake. To attach small pieces of clay to each other, wet the surface a bit so they will stick.

Bake on cookie sheets lined with old foil or coated with non-stick finish. (Be sure to save the foil to use again and again!)

Cookie-type projects bake at 300° F for about 30 minutes. Projects that are 1/2" – 2" thick need to bake at 300° F for at least an hour. If an item browns too quickly, cover with used foil and finish baking.

If you're happy with the warm, light brown color of your baked project, just finish it with a coat of sealer, such as acrylic finishes, acrylic floor wax, or clear nail polish. Tempera, water colors, or marking pens can be used to decorate baked items.

CRAYON REVIVAL ★ ★ ★ ★ ★ ★ ★

Recycle your old crayons by melting them down and making beautiful new ones — even crayons with swirls of color!

MATERIALS

Old crayons

Paper cupcake liners

Soup can

Saucepan

Muffin tin

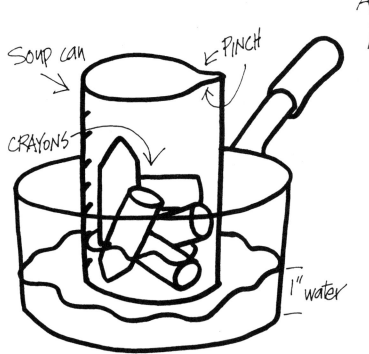

Soup can → PINCH

CRAYONS

1" water

Ask a grown-up to melt crayons in can heated in 1" hot water.

Pour melted crayon in paper liner.

Pop out when cooled.

Peel off all the paper, and sort crayons by color. Fill a saucepan with 1" – 2" of water. Pinch the top of a clean soup can to create a sort of pouring spout. Fill the can half full with broken crayons. Ask an adult to heat the saucepan, never going higher than medium heat. *The wax in the crayons is flammable, so don't let it get too hot. Because of the danger involved in using hot wax, a grown-up must do the melting and pouring of the wax.* Crayons melt at a very low temperature, and if the heat is kept low, everything will go safely and smoothly. You can do the peeling, sorting, and breaking up of the crayons, as well as the testing of the final product!

After heating for a few minutes, the crayons will be melted to a liquid wax. Have a grown-up carefully pour the wax into paper-lined muffin tins. Pour about 1/2" of melted crayon into each paper cup. You can add a swirl of another color wax or let cool and add another layer of a different color. Let cool. You can hurry the cooling by placing the muffin tin in the freezer for a few minutes, or setting it outdoors on a cold day. Peel the paper away when the crayon is cooled and solid.

Candy molds can be used to make all kinds of clever crayon shapes. Many fun shapes are available from the Wilton Company, from dinosaurs to cartoon characters. Better yet, save old plastic wrapping materials from candy, make-up, and toys, to use as molds. The hardened crayons pop out easily and the molds can be used over and over.

3

CREATING WITH THE EARTH'S BOUNTY

TEXTURES

We enjoy art with more than just our eyes. While creating we can use our senses of touch and smell as well. Natural materials are so much fun to work with because they stimulate our fingers as we work with them. The smooth coolness of a pebble or shell, or the crunchy stiffness of cornhusks feels unusual as we work with them. When collecting or preparing materials, take time to squish the soft mud or to smell the dried grasses. These sensations will come back to you again and again as you enjoy your finished artwork in the months to come. Long after you return from the beach or the mountains, you can take out your creations and relive your nature experience.

Nature provides us with many different textures: smooth like a stone, rough like tree bark, slick like a wet shell, spongy like moss, prickly like a pod, soft like a flower petal. Let your fingers enjoy the feel of natural materials, giving you ideas about how best to create with these earthly treasures.

VINE VASE

This project creates a very unusual vase and recycles glass jars or cans.

MATERIALS ✹✹🕯

Clean glass jar, bottle, or juice can

Vine: several lengths of thin vine with leaves removed (grape, honeysuckle, clematis, or similar vines)

Sturdy scissors

Tacky-type glue

Turn the jar upside-down and wrap vine around it.

If you don't have vines, any flexible plant material can be tried: reeds, thick grass or flower stems, straw or cornhusks.

Turn the jar upside-down and begin at the base. With spots of glue, begin wrapping vine around and around the jar. Keep it tight and close together so the jar doesn't show. As you come to the end of a length of vine, snip the end neatly at a slant, glue down, and hold in place until the glue sticks. Then glue down the next piece. Keep going until you have covered most of the jar. Then turn it right side up and finish wrapping.

The top wrap can be decorated by attaching a different color or texture of vine, a ring of nuts or pebbles, or tiny pine cones (hemlock cones are perfect) with glue.

You need to be patient while waiting for the glue to dry. A piece of old pantyhose can be secured around the finished vase to hold the vines in place while the glue dries completely.

To preserve the finished vase, you can brush on a coat of clear acrylic finish, or acrylic floor wax.

Use cans for bases, creating pencil holders or desk sets that are all wrapped with similar plant materials.

BASIC BASKETS

MATERIALS

Assorted natural fibers: grasses, yucca, wheat, willow, straw, jute, cornhusks, weeds, raffia — whatever you can find. Look around the edges of your yard, along the sides of pathways and roads, wherever plants aren't mowed or sprayed. You can purchase materials at craft supply stores, too.

Reusables: yarn, string, ribbon, embroidery threads, fabric strips — any or all can be used.

Box for a base: a round box like an ice cream container is best. Or, you can use the pattern provided; just trace it onto some cardboard and cut it out.

Masking tape

Scissors

If you are using a round ice cream container, discard the top and cut slits on the sides about 1" apart, right down to the base. Be sure that you end up with an uneven number of strips. If you are using the pattern, trace onto paper and cut out; then, draw onto cardboard, flip pattern piece over, and draw again to create one rounded pattern. Cut out. Fold the sections up at the base to make the basket form.

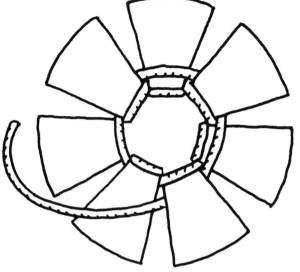

Weave the yarn over and under the basket form.

Shape the sides of the basket as you weave.

Start weaving your fiber strips at the bottom, securing the end of the first piece of fiber inside the basket with masking tape. Weave different pieces of fiber over and under the cardboard strips, adding new or different types of fiber as you go. When you add another piece, weave it over the end of the last piece you used, to hide the end.

Continue weaving over and under, working up the side of the basket as you go. Weave up to about 1/2" from the end of the basket frame. Fold the cardboard ends back and tuck them into the weaving; then finish the last rows, hiding the cardboard ends with them.

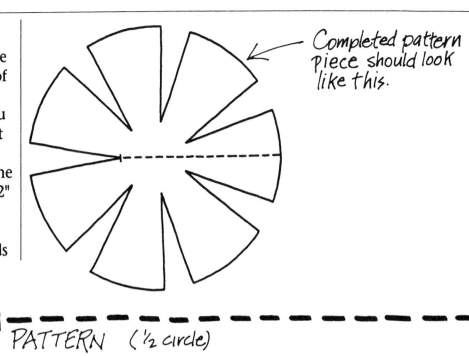

Completed pattern piece should look like this.

PATTERN (½ circle)

BARK WEAVING

MATERIALS

Slab of tree bark from a log on the ground, or an old weathered board (Don't peel bark off a living tree.)

Nails (1/2" – 3/4" in length, with small heads)

Assorted fibers to weave: cornhusks, grasses, feathers, strips of leather or fabric

Yarn

Scissors and hammer

Have you ever looked very closely at the bark of a tree? Isn't it amazing with all of its bumps and lumps? Now look at another tree. See any differences? Some bark is smooth, some is very rough, and some even looks like it is about to fall off!

A tree's bark acts very much like your skin does for you. It keeps bugs and disease from entering the tree. It protects the tree from the ravages of weather and forest fire. The bark thickens as a tree grows. It provides hiding places for butterflies to lay eggs and nesting holes for small birds. Mosses and fungi grow on it's bumpy surface.

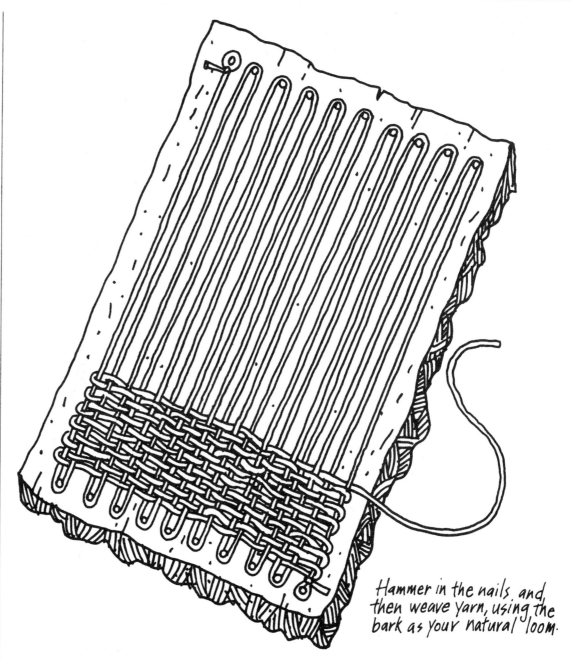

Hammer in the nails, and then weave yarn, using the bark as your natural loom.

Work in the natural materials and leave finished weaving on the bark.

When looking for bark for a project, be careful to never pull or cut bark from a living tree. It will let disease enter the tree, and may eventually kill it. Search for your bark on the ground or pull it off a fallen log.

Once you have found a flat piece of bark with an interesting shape, begin hammering a row of nails along one end of the bark. Hammer another row directly opposite at the other end. Knot one end of a length of yarn around the first nail and wind the yarn back and forth between the two rows of nails, looping around each nail. This will be the *warp* for your weaving.

Weave in the fibers (grasses, cornhusks, yarn, etc.) by manipulating the yarn and fibers with your fingers. Continue an over-under pattern across the warp, reversing at the end and returning on the next row.

If working with yarn as your fiber, you might enjoy working with a yarn needle, which makes the weaving much easier. (See page 27 for instructions.) If you choose not to use a needle, the yarn end can be wrapped with tape to stiffen it for easier handling.

Leave the finished weaving in place on the bark or board. Tuck ends of fibers back inside the weaving to hide them. Dried flowers, feathers, and bits of moss can be tucked into the weaving or glued on to make it even more interesting.

CORNHUSKS

Cornhusks are interesting and fun to work with because they can be crunched or stretched into a variety of shapes. They can be rolled and tied, or wet and shaped, or curled. They can be left natural, or painted, or dyed. They act as nature's packaging, keeping the corn moist and sweet. Native Americans used the husks to weave clothing or wrap foods for cooking. Perhaps you have eaten a tamale, a Mexican food steamed in cornhusks.

If you can't obtain husks from a farm or garden, you may want to buy them from a craft supply store. If you purchase fresh corn in the husk, you can save the husks by letting them air dry completely, and then storing in a box in the garage, until you're ready to work with them.

To soften cornhusks for easier working, add three teaspoons of glycerin (from any drugstore) to a dishpan full of water. Soak the husks for a few minutes, and then lay on a folded towel, ready to use.

Cornhusk Dolls

MATERIALS ✿ ✿ ✿

12 husks (soak in water a few minutes)

Rubber bands, yarn, or string

Scissors

Lay about 6 husks on top of each other. Gather and wrap a rubber band tightly about an inch from one end. Pull the ends back over the banded area and fasten with another rubber band. This makes the head.

To make the arms, roll 2 husks together lengthwise in a tight roll. Fasten with 2 rubber bands near the ends. Slip this arm section inside the body husks, below the neck. Fasten

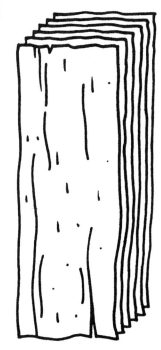

Stack 6 husks.

Wrap a band 1" from the end.

Pull ends back over the band and fasten with another band. This makes the head.

the arms in place by wrapping some yarn, string, or a rubber band, in a crisscross across the body top.

Trim the bottom of the husks evenly to create a skirt. If you want legs or pants, separate the husks in 2 sections and wrap each leg section tightly at the ankle with a rubber band or string.

You can glue cornsilk, twine, yarn, or moss to the head for hair.

Roll 2 husks to make arms.

Slide the arms inside the body.

Fasten in place by tying string in a crisscross pattern across the chest.

3-D Cornhusk Collage

MATERIALS

Cornhusks

Glue (see page 24)

Cardboard or tagboard

Scissors

Draw the image you want onto the cardboard. Trim and shape small pieces of husks, and then glue to the cardboard.

Because cornhusks can be curled on a pencil while wet, or shredded, or twisted, they can become 3-dimensional collages where parts stick out from the cardboard. Tacks can hold pieces in place until the glue dries. Add seeds or beans and let your imagination go.

WALL PLAQUE

MATERIALS

Slab of tree bark (from a log on the ground, not from a living tree)

Assorted decorative items: dry moss, leaves, seed pods, feathers, cones, shells, weeds

Tacky-type glue

Thin wire

Lay the piece of bark on your work area and decide which side is more appealing; then, lay out the leaves, moss, and other things you gathered, until you have arranged something interesting. You may want to create an image, such as a bird or flower arrangement, or you may want to make a collage of the various textures and colors you have gathered.

Glue the items in place. When dry, attach the thin wire to the back for hanging. You can also nail or glue on a loop cut from a soda pop six-pack holder to make a hanging loop.

STICKS & STONES

Stones are one of the natural materials you can find just about anywhere you live. Formed millions of years ago, they were made by volcanic eruptions, or by the settling of ancient ocean bottoms under heat and pressure. Stones have many different textures, from shiny to gritty. If you have a smooth, rounded stone, it was probably worn smooth by the flow of a river or stream for thousands of years. While stones can be found everywhere, some stones are so unusual or have such beautiful colors that they are treasured. We use them for jewelry and call them precious stones. Some stones are very hard and can be cut with a diamond saw into shapes that sparkle when they reflect light. We call these cut stones gems.

Look carefully while searching for stones, and you may find a real fossil which is the remains or imprint of a living creature, left in stone. The actual bone or shell dissolved over time as water and mineral salts filled the imprint and turned to stone. Fossils take millions of years to form.

PEBBLE TRIVET & COASTERS ♥ ⌒ ♥ ⌒ ♥ ⌒ ♥

MATERIALS

Small, smooth, flat pebbles

Quart-jar lid for each coaster
(such as mayonnaise jar lid)

Large metal lid for each trivet
(ask a restaurant to save one for you
or use some other suitable base)

Plaster of Paris and mixing tools

You can make a single trivet or a whole set of matching coasters to set hot or cold drinks on.

Ask a grown-up to help mix the plaster, following package directions. When it begins to thicken, spoon it into the jar lids, filling each lid half full.

Select pretty pebbles and press them into the plaster before it hardens, filling the area inside the jar lid with stones. You may want to create a design, if you have different colors and sizes of pebbles. Plaster may squeeze up and out of the lid, but it can be wiped away later. Let the plaster harden; then use old socks or pieces of old towels to rub away any plaster that covers the tops of the stones.

Brush a coat of acrylic finish or acrylic floor wax over the plaster and stones to give your trivet a shiny finish. You may want to glue some felt scraps to bottoms of the coasters to prevent scratches on furniture.

Whales have been washed ashore with up to fifty plastic bags inside their guts. Plastic bags should never be left on the beach.

NATURE NOTE

Make one large trivet
or several small ones.

STONE CRITTERS ♥ ∧ ∨ ∧ ∨ ∧ ♥ ∧ ♥ ∧ ♥ ∧ ♥ ∧ ♥ ∨

MATERIALS

Rounded stones in assorted shapes and sizes

Acrylic paints or permanent marker pens

Adhesive: Tacky-type glue, silicone sealer (sold in tubes in hardware stores).

The Navajos use colored sands as well as crushed charcoal and other materials to make elaborate paintings for healing and ceremonial purposes.

ART SPEAK

Rinse the stones and let dry. Then lay them out, looking at their shapes and colors to get ideas. You can use them to create paperweights, doorstops, garden sculpture, refrigerator magnets, or interesting designs.

Tiny decorated pebbles can be glued to magnets, pin backs, or barrettes.

To fasten stones together to create animal ears, arms, or legs, dab silicone sealer or tacky-type glue on the stone. Hold stones in place until the glue sets.

Use paints or permanent markers to decorate or draw on eyes and mouth. Glue broom straws, dry grass, or toothpicks on for whiskers. Old leather scraps make good ears or tongues.

Large rocks can be painted like ladybugs or turtles and placed in your garden.

DALMATION PUP

Use white stones. Make black spots with paint or marker or glue on tiny, dark pebbles. Glue on yarn tail.

OWL

Paint circles and triangles for eyes and nose. Use marking pen to draw feathers or find feathers and glue on.

LADYBUG

Paint large rocks in bright colors. Position them around your yard or garden.

MATERIALS

Fine sand

Glue

White tagboard: good reusable sources are gift boxes, shirt cardboard, and old file folders.

Cotton swabs

Did you know there is pink sand, pure white sand, along with darker shades of brown and grey sand? Sand is made by wind and water wearing away rocks over many, many years. It is truly one of nature's wonders. Some sand is coarse on your feet and some is as soft as baby powder.

Collect sand, keeping different colors separate, or tint your sand with natural dyes (see page 16) or food coloring. To tint, place sand in separate jars, and then add a few drops of coloring to each jar. Prepare or collect several different shades of sand.

Use the cotton swabs to paint a design with glue on the tagboard. Sprinkle the sand onto the wet glue, using the different colors to get different effects. Let dry and shake off the excess sand.

You can glue on bits of dried flowers and weeds to make your sand art even more interesting.

Sand, shells, and pebbles go together naturally, so if you want to create a frame for your sand painting, collect small shells or pebbles, and glue around the outside edge of your picture. Thick craft glue, or silicone sealer will hold the shells down securely.

Make a decorative frame for your sand art with pebbles, shells, or acorns.

SAND CLAY SCULPTURE ♡ ∧ ♡ ∧ ♡ ∧ ♡ ∧ ♡ ∧ ♡ ∧ ♡ ∧ ♡ ∧

MATERIALS 🍁

2 cups fine sand

1 cup water

1 cup cornstarch

Saucepan and spoon

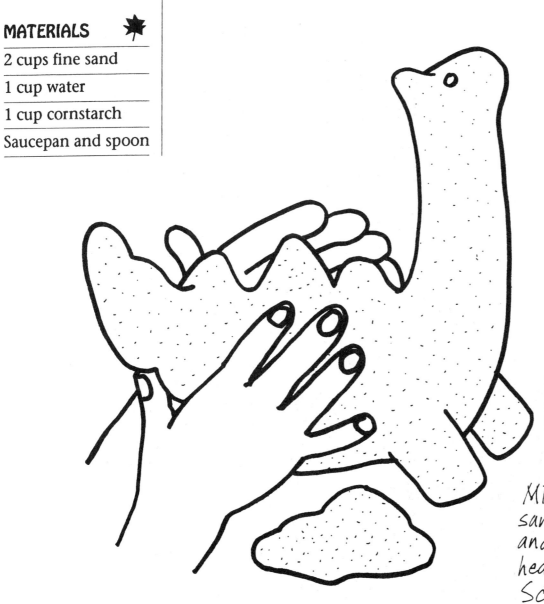

Mix together the sand, cornstarch, and water; then heat. Let cool. Sculpt!

Make clay from sand! Mix sand, cornstarch, and water in a saucepan. If you want to add color, stir in drops of food coloring or natural dyes (see page 16). Ask a grown-up to help you cook over medium heat, stirring constantly.

When your mixture thickens, remove from the heat. Carefully pour it into a dish, and let it cool. If you drape a wet washcloth or towel over the clay, it will cool more quickly. Use your fingers and a stick or spoon to sculpt it into whatever you choose. It will get very hard when dry.

This clay makes interesting small animals or pots. You can also make your own "fossils" by pressing bones (saved from your dinner), leaves, or feathers into the moist clay, then removing them and letting it dry.

LOG PENCIL HOLDER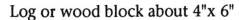

MATERIALS

Log or wood block about 4"x 6"

Sandpaper

Scrap of felt or other soft fabric

Glue

Hand drill (rotary, not electric):
Use a drill bit that will make an
opening large enough for a pencil

Hammer and nail

Scissors

Vermont has approximately 18
billion live trees in its forests.
That's 32,000 for each man,
woman, and child living in the
state.

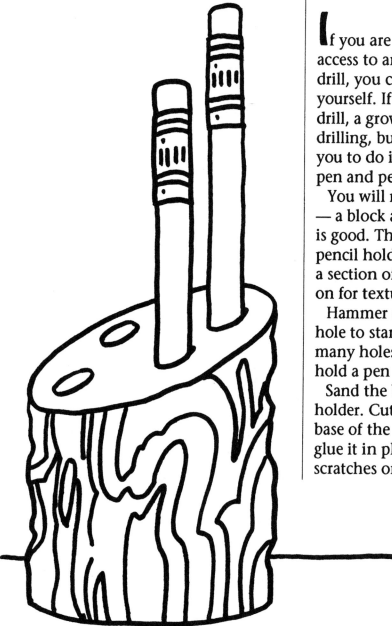

If you are lucky enough to have access to an old-fashioned hand drill, you can drill the holes yourself. If you have an electric drill, a grown-up must do the drilling, but there is plenty for you to do in making this great pen and pencil holder.

You will need a piece of wood — a block about 4" – 6" in size is good. The most interesting pencil holders can be made from a section of log. Leave the bark on for texture.

Hammer a nail in to create a hole to start the drill. Make as many holes as you like; each will hold a pen or pencil.

Sand the bottom of the pencil holder. Cut the felt to fit the base of the pencil holder and glue it in place to prevent scratches on any furniture.

TWIG ANIMALS ♥ ⌄ ♥ ⌄ ♥ ⌄ ♥ ⌄ ♥ ⌄ ♥

MATERIALS ✹✹✹

Thin willow twigs, about 15" long

Little twig animals like these were made by the ancestors of today's Native Americans. Perhaps the twig animals were associated with hunting. Perhaps they were just for fun! Since archaeologists date them as 2,500 years old, we'll never know for certain.

Now, you can make a collection of your own twig animals from long, thin willow or cottonwood twigs. Isn't it amazing how flexible a twig can be?

Pull the twig apart up to the end, leaving it joined for about 1/2" (1). Bend about 1" from the end to make the back legs (2). Bend the rest of the twig as shown, wrapping the final part around the neck and tucking the end inside the neck.

Make several of these wonderful animals to "roam" a bookshelf or tabletop together.

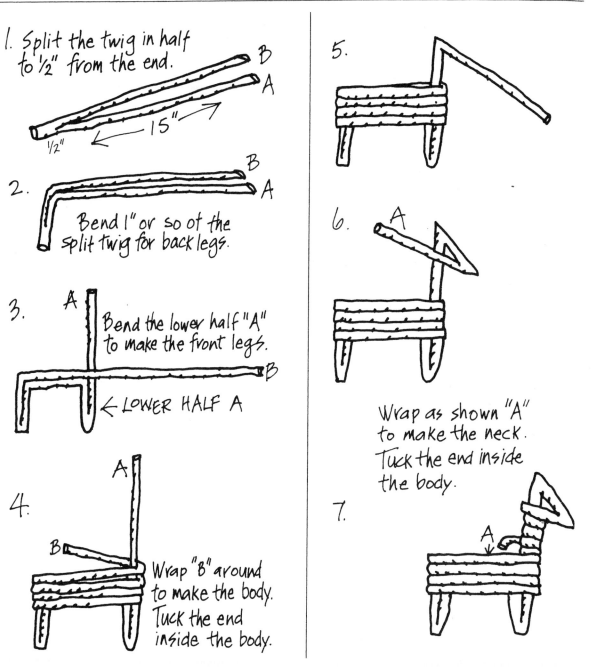

1. Split the twig in half to ½" from the end.

2. Bend 1" or so of the split twig for back legs.

3. Bend the lower half "A" to make the front legs.
←LOWER HALF A

4. Wrap "B" around to make the body. Tuck the end inside the body.

5.

6. Wrap as shown "A" to make the neck. Tuck the end inside the body.

7.

DRIFTWOOD SCULPTURE ♥∧♥∧♥∧♥∧♥∧♥∧♥∧♥∧

MATERIALS

Driftwood in assorted small sizes and shapes

Adhesive: Tacky glue, silicone sealer, or hot glue gun (for grown-up use)

Driftwood is abundant near the seashore, but don't think you have to live near the beach to find it. Look along the banks of a river, lake, or stream, and you will find lots of interesting pieces. While you're out collecting, look for interesting shells, stones, and other things that you can add to your sculpture, or save to use on another project.

Clean the driftwood by rubbing it with an old towel or brush. Select your pieces carefully, looking for unusual twists or shapes in the wood. Some pieces look like animals or pieces of modern art without even adding anything to them — truly nature's work of art!

Choose a flat piece to be the base. Build up from there adding pieces as you like, gluing securely before adding the next piece. Feel free to add other natural objects to your sculp-

ture, such as pebbles, shells, feathers, grasses, or dried flowers.

Sometimes pieces will go together and remind you of a bird, animal, or person. Other times, your sculpture may not look like anything you've seen before! You will have created something out of nothing.

A tree takes in about 20 pounds of carbon dioxide each year. It gives off enough oxygen to keep four people breathing for a year.

Some pieces of driftwood sculpture may look like things you've seen; others will be entirely free-form.

PEBBLE JEWELRY

MATERIALS

Small pebbles or pretty rocks

Tacky glue

Jewelry backings from some old jewelry or craft store

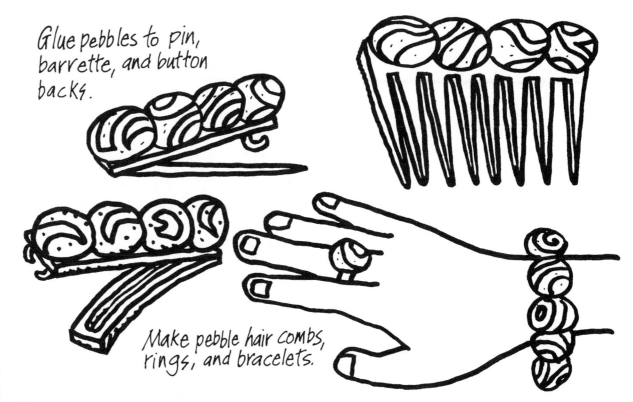

Glue pebbles to pin, barrette, and button backs.

Make pebble hair combs, rings, and bracelets.

NATURAL WONDERS

Trees existed more than 200 million years ago and are the largest form of life ever to inhabit the earth.

Search around your house for some inexpensive pin backs, earring backs, barrettes, and hair combs. Ask if you can use them first! If not, you can buy backings at craft shops. Button backs from fabric-covered button kits (at the fabric store) can be used to make pebble buttons.

Collect some pretty, small pebbles. Wash them and let dry. Select interesting pebble combinations and glue them to the jewelry backs.

When the glue dries, you can decorate the pebbles with fine-tip marking pens, making designs or faces, or leave them their natural colors.

Brush on a coat of clear nail polish to give the pebbles a shine, as if they just came from the stream bed. What other things can you make by gluing carefully selected pebbles or shells onto backings made from yogurt containers or tissue rolls? What about napkin rings, bracelets, vases for violets, ...

TWIG WEAVINGS ♥ ∧ ♥ ∧ ♥ ∧ ♥ ∧ ♥ ∧ ♥ ∧ ♥ ∧ ♥

MATERIALS ✿✿

Small twigs, or branches, with a forked or twisted shape

Yarn scraps

Feathers, leaves, cattails, pods — for trim

Searching for an interesting twig is the most important part of this project.

> Each year a tree puts on a new layer of trunk. These layers form rings in the tree's trunk. We can tell how old a tree is by counting the rings —one per year of growth. Rings are narrow during years of drought, and may even show the marks of a forest fire that passed through.

NATURE NOTE

Search for an interesting branch to be the loom for the weaving. As you look, you will notice that no two branches are exactly alike. Different types of trees and bushes have different textures and shapes in their branches as well. Some will be slender and delicate, others stubby and chunky. As you search, think about how carefully a bird searches for just the right branch to weave a nest on.

You don't have to break branches from living trees. Just look about you on the ground, especially after a storm when rain and wind have knocked them to the ground.

Weave the yarns back and forth between the branched twigs in a pattern. The yarn will resemble a spider web a bit. Stick feathers, leaves, or pods and cones in between the yarn to make your weaving more interesting. Hang your finished weaving on a wall or lean it against a bookcase or on the mantle.

SAND CASTING

MATERIALS

Used plastic milk jug or half-gallon milk carton

Fine sand and water

Plaster of Paris and stirrer

Assorted objects to cast: seed pods, stones, shells, leaves, twigs

Sand has long been used as a way of molding shapes that are then filled with liquids such as molten metals or melted wax.

ART SPEAK

You can make sand castings right where the sand is — at a beach, a playground, or even your own backyard sandbox.

You will need to wet the sand with water first; then use your hands to dig a shallow hole. Pat the sand to smooth it. Press seed pods, shells, or rocks and driftwood pieces into the moist sand. Leave them in place, making sure the sand is smooth around the base of each object.

Cut the plastic jug or milk carton in half. Mix the plaster in it following the directions on the package.

When the plaster begins to thicken, pour it carefully and gently over the objects to cast. It will be like thick cake batter. Pour on more plaster until it is about 1" – 2" deep. It should be thick enough that it won't spread out on the sand too much. Let it harden and dry.

Go for a walk or clean up the beach while you wait about half an hour. Then, carefully lift up the hardened plaster and gently brush the loose sand away with your hand.

Plaster casts can also be made of designs drawn in the wet sand with your finger or a stick.

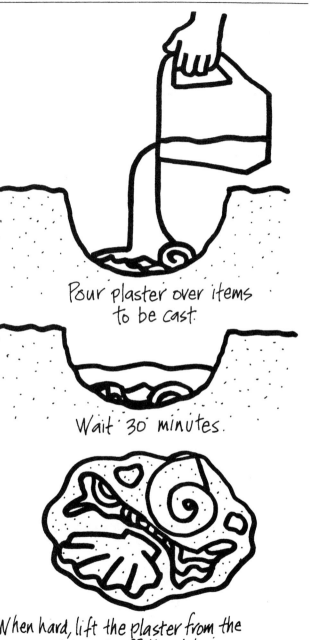

Pour plaster over items to be cast.

Wait 30 minutes.

When hard, lift the plaster from the sand and brush off the debris.

TWIG PICTURE FRAME ♥ ⌄ ♥ ⌄ ♥ ⌄ ♥ ⌄ ♥ ⌄ ♥ ⌄ ♥ ⌄ ♥

MATERIALS ✹✹

Cardboard

Twigs

Glue

Scissors

Cut cardboard to the desired size. Brown cardboard from boxes is best; you can paint it as you desire.

Break twigs to fit the frame and glue in place around the edges. Tiny acorns, pine cones, nuts, and dried flowers can be glued on for accents.

Glue your photograph or drawing into the frame with rubber cement.

To hang the frame from a wall, ask a grown-up to hot glue a pop top from a soda can to the back of the frame.

If you want the frame to stand upright on a table top, cut a support from cardboard, bend it at one end, and glue to the back of the frame.

Cut a cardboard shape large enough to support your frame.

Fold one end back (on dotted line) and glue to the back of the frame.

BIRD FEEDERS

It's always fun to make something useful, but it's even more fun to watch what you've made being used by a living creature. Birds live all around us, no matter if we're in the city or the country. Making a bird feeder can bring them up close to you for observation and enjoyment. And what a great way to reuse what might have been trash!

Bird feeders can be made from just about anything you have around that can be hung or set out off the ground, ready to hold a supply of birdseed, while hungry birds dig in for a meal!

Birds like to eat where they are safe. You may be feeding ground feeders, such as pigeons or doves. They like to be able to see around them several feet to be certain that nothing is preying on them. Keep their feeders away from shrubbery. When setting your hanging feeders out, take care to place them away from tree branches or fences where cats can position themselves. You don't want your bird feeders to become cat feeders!

Milk Carton Feeder

Materials

Clean milk carton

2' of heavy string

12" long stick or dowel

Scissors

Use the scissors to cut away the carton as shown. Insert the stick in the bottom portion, letting it make a perch on 2 sides for birds to sit on as they dig through the seeds.

Cut or punch a hole to insert the string for hanging.

Jug Bird Feeder

Materials

Gallon plastic jug

Wire, string, or leather strip, 12" long

Stick or dowel, about 12" long

Scissors and nail

Cut away the sides and top of the jug, leaving a base of about 1 1/2".

Poke 2 holes in the plastic with the nail, using scissors or a knife to enlarge the hole if needed. Push the stick through the holes, so it pokes out both sides to give the birds a perch.

Poke 2 holes through the top and insert the wire or string.

Pine Cone Feeder and More

Materials ✴

Pine cone or tissue tube

Peanut butter and birdseed

Corrugated cardboard

String, about 12"

Table knife or Popsicle stick

Shallow pan

Pine Cone Feeder

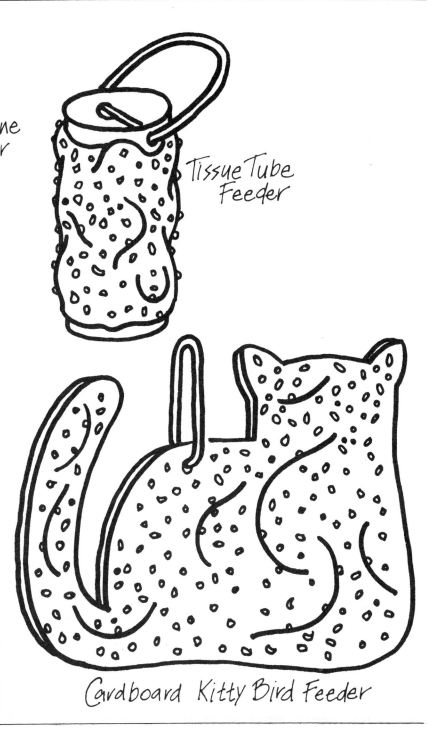

Tissue Tube Feeder

Use the knife or stick to spread peanut butter all over the pine cone. Be sure to spread between the scales of the cone, too.

Place a layer of birdseed in the pan and roll the cone in the seed, until all the peanut butter is covered with birdseed. Tie the string around one end of the pine cone and hang it from a tree branch.

If you don't have pine cones, you can do the same thing with a toilet tissue tube. Punch 2 holes in one end (opposite each other), and thread a string through for hanging. Spread with peanut butter and roll in birdseed.

If you want to get even more creative, use old corrugated cardboard boxes to draw clever shapes — perhaps a cat outline. Ask a grown-up to help you cut the shapes out of the cardboard using a serrated knife, like a steak knife, or a craft knife. Punch a hole in the top to tie string through. Spread the cardboard shape with peanut butter and dip in birdseed.

Cardboard Kitty Bird Feeder

EARTHWORM WONDERLAND

Materials ✦✦

Large glass jar: choose one with a wide mouth and a metal lid

Soda pop can

Soft, damp soil

Black construction paper

Colored chalks

Tape

Nail and hammer

This project looks like a beautiful piece of decorative artwork, but lift the decorated paper ring and you can view earthworms hard at work.

Worms help turn garbage into soil, and they keep the soil loose and aerated by burrowing through it. They make soil by taking in the compost (food and yard clippings) and dirt, then pushing it out their tail. The dirt that comes out of the worms, called castings, is soft and very fine — perfect for gardening!

To help you study these fascinating, hard-working worms indoors, make a pretty home for them from an old, used, large glass jar. Borrow a few earthworms from your garden soil, but, when you are finished studying them, be sure to return them to your garden, yard, or a park, where they can continue their good work for the earth.

Put the soda pop can, open end down, inside the jar. Carefully spoon moist soil around the can, so the can stays in the center and the soil fills the area around it. (The can keeps the worms from always staying in the center of the jar where you can't see them.)

Once the jar is full of soil, the worms can be added. If you have a good spot to dig them in your yard, borrow a handful and put them in the jar. They will burrow down into the soil within a few minutes. If you need to buy worms, they can be purchased wherever fishing supplies are sold. You can get different types and sizes of worms; Red Wigglers are small and lively and won't crowd the jar. Don't put too many in — about a dozen is plenty for a gallon jar. Punch a few holes in the jar lid with the hammer and nail, so the worms get a good supply of oxygen.

Keep the soil lightly moist, but not wet. Don't let it dry out or the worms will dry out, too. To feed them, sprinkle on crushed, dry dog food or bits of shredded carrot peels. Worms also like coffee grounds and cornmeal.

Worms like darkness, just like under the ground. Cut the black paper to fit around the jar. Use colored chalks to decorate it with interesting designs. Draw on only one side of the paper.

Tape the ends of the paper together to make a ring that fits around the jar. Slide it up when you want to watch the worms, slide it back down over the glass when you are finished. They will burrow next to the glass so you will see them better. Notice how quickly they burrow away from the light when you are watching them.

When you are through studying them, turn them loose in your yard or at a park, putting them under a bit of sod or in some loose soil in a shady spot. They will burrow down below the surface and make a new home there.

PAPER SHADE

SOIL
(fill the jar)

SODA POP CAN

WORMS
(about 12)

ANT RANCH

Ants are fascinating little creatures. They are fun to watch. The next time you find a trail of the little creatures entering your house, make an ant ranch and invite them in.

Materials ✹✹

Large glass jar with a screw-on lid

Smaller jar with a lid or crushed aluminum foil ball

Pantyhose

Rubber band

Sandy soil

Hammer and nail

Punch some holes in the jar lid with the nail and hammer, so the ants will have air to breathe. Set aside.

Put the smaller jar or a clump of wadded, used aluminum foil into the larger jar. This will keep the ants from making their home in the center of the jar (where you can't watch them). Fill the area around the aluminum foil ball with soft sand or soil. Put a few drops of water on the soil. Ants need some water to drink, so be sure the soil doesn't dry out

The foil ball is covered with sand. Put a piece of pantyhose over the top and screw the lid on tight.

too much. Add a few drops of water each week.

When the soil is ready, add the ants. Ants are easy to find. Look for them along a sidewalk. You can use a pencil to make catching them easier. Point the pencil down to the ground, in front of an ant. It will climb up the pencil point. Hold the pencil over your ant ranch and gently push the ant off the pencil. It helps to have someone with you who can put the lid on the jar so the ants don't get away. Try to get at least 20 ants, so you have plenty to watch.

Warning! Be sure to get all your ants from the same place. If you get ants from different groups, they will kill each other.

Screw the lid on, and then, to keep the ants from escaping, fasten a piece of old pantyhose over the lid with a rubber band.

Finding food for ants is easy. They don't eat very much. One crumb of cornflake or a couple of grains of sugar is all they need. They get sick and die if they eat too much. Watch them, and when they are out of food, drop in another crumb or two. When you are done studying your ant guests, return them to where you found them.

Print with a pencil eraser,

or print with your fingertip.

After you have noticed the delicate shape and movements of your ants, you may want to make some ant prints to decorate notepaper or make cartoons with.

Use a black inked stamp pad and press your fingertips into the ink, then print with them to create ant bodies. Draw on the legs and antennae with a black pen. If you want to print with black paint, use the eraser end of a pencil to print the bodies of the ants, and draw on the detail with a fine-tip black pen. They look cute running across a notecard or decorating a book cover.

GOLDFISH BOWL

Materials

Gallon plastic jug

Heavy scissors

Permanent markers or stickers

To make a simple bowl for a single goldfish or guppy to live in, just cut a clean plastic jug in half. Wash away the label and decorate with bright colored permanent markers or stickers. Add a few interesting rocks and shells for your fish to explore.

Fill with lukewarm tap water. Let the tap water sit for a few hours or overnight so any chlorine will evaporate away, before you put your goldfish in. Your fish will need a tiny bit of food each day. Use breadcrumbs or purchase fish food.

It's fun to watch your fish move gracefully through the water. Perhaps you'd like to sketch it or use watercolors to create a painting of it as you watch.

Change the water every few days, when it begins to look cloudy, or if your fish tries to gulp air from the water's surface. Be sure to let the fresh water sit a bit to evaporate chlorine each time you refill the fish bowl.

ANIMAL TRACK PAPERWEIGHT

Materials

Plaster of Paris

Jug of water

Large can or cut-down jug to mix plaster in and stick to stir

Raccoon

Snowshoe Rabbit

Deer

Stir the plaster with a stick. When it gets thick, pour it over a track. Let harden, then gently lift up the plaster cast.

First you have to locate some animal tracks to use. It's best right after a rain or after the ground has been irrigated. Look for firm, but soft mud with clear tracks that show up well.

If you are in the forest, look for tracks of wild animals near a pond, trail, or road. If you are visiting a beach or a park, look for bird tracks or dog paw prints.

As you study the prints, notice how they were made.

If they were spaced closely, the animal was moving slowly. If the tracks are far apart, the animal was moving more quickly, taking longer strides. You can tell how large or heavy an animal is by the size of its track. It's easy to tell a fawn's tracks from those of an adult deer. The fawn's are smaller, closer together, and aren't pressed as far down into the mud. Isn't that the same with people?

If you can't find animal tracks, look for interesting tire tracks, or footprints. You can even do this project in your kitchen, with a dishpan full of mud, and a cooperative dog or cat to make the prints. If you don't have a pet, try your own footprints or handprints!

Now, follow the instructions on the package of plaster of Paris. Once it thickens, pour the plaster

onto the print, letting some plaster surround the print. (If it is too runny, wait a few more minutes, until the plaster becomes thicker.)

The plaster will become solid enough to pick up in a few minutes. When it is hard, gently lift it up from the mud and put it in a sunny spot or indoors to dry. Brush any dirt away that sticks to the plaster. Let the cast sit overnight to dry harder.

It's fun to make a collection of casts from various animals. The casts can be used as book ends, paperweights, door stops, or as sculpture. Glue a piece of soft felt or flannel to the bottom of the plaster to protect furniture. If you want to paint the cast, use natural dyes (see page 16), tempera, latex paint, or watercolors. Seal with a waterproof finish if desired.

SHELL BUTTERFLY MAGNETS

Materials ✹✹

Pairs of shells: mussel, clam, or oyster can be used

Antennae can be: twigs, broom straws, or pipe cleaner

Length of thread and scissors

Paint or markers

Tacky-type glue

If you have a chance, study a real butterfly closely, as it sits on a flower, but please don't touch it. Notice the wings are identical and how the designs create abstract sections of color and pattern. Moths have fascinating color patterns on their wings, too.

The coloration on butterflies and moths actually protects them in their environment. Butterflies have bright coloring that hides them as they feed at flower blossoms. Moths tend to have coloring that matches the bark of trees, where they can blend in and hide from birds, who think they are a tasty snack!

Now create an interesting butterfly or moth to attach to a magnet and mounted on the refrigerator. If you like, glue the finished butterflies to barrettes, or jewelry brooch backings. You can also tie a thread around the middle of your butterfly and hang from the ceiling to create a mobile.

Paint or decorate the shells with butterfly designs, decorating both sides alike. Let the swirls and texture of the shells inspire you. Cut the twig or pipe cleaner to make two antennae. Glue into position.

BUG GUEST HOUSE

Materials ✹✹

1 quart milk carton

Old pantyhose and rubber band

Heavy scissors or craft knife

Old magazines and glue

Ladybugs in California migrate to the mountains to hibernate for the winter.

NATURE NOTE

A bug guest house is the perfect way to get a close-up view, without harming the insect. Keep the insect or caterpillar just long enough to observe behavior and then return it to the wild, where you found it.

Be sure to put in whatever plant material your bug needs for food. Sprinkle a few drops of water on the leaves or bottom of the house.

To make the house, cut two window openings on the sides of the carton. Look through the magazines for colorful pictures. Trim and glue them to cover the milk carton, making a collage of interesting and beautiful pictures of nature.

When the glue is dry, cut off a leg from the pantyhose and pull it up over the box, having the toe at the base of the carton. Add your bug, some plant material, and a few drops of water. Then, pull the pantyhose up tightly, and trim, leaving about 3" to tie in a knot or fasten snugly with a rubber band. Watch your bug for a few hours or overnight, and then set it free. Save your bug house for another guest!

BIRD CAFÉ

Bird Cupcakes

Materials ✹

1/2 cup peanut butter

1 cup birdseed

2 1/2 cups cornmeal

1/2 cup melted shortening

Muffin tin (greased)

Sticks: the size of a pencil

Yarn

Combine the ingredients in a large bowl. Stir together. Drop the mixture into the muffin cups, pressing it down with your fingers. To create a hole for hanging, push a stick down in the middle. Let dry. Remove from the pan and take out the sticks. Thread yarn through the hole. Tie a loop and hang from a tree for the birds to enjoy.

Bird Bell

Materials ✹✹

Small yogurt container or paper cup

Ingredients as listed in Bird Cupcakes

Yarn

Cardboard circle, about 2" in diameter (a cereal box would be good for this)

Nail or sharp pencil

Prepare the ingredients as described in Bird Cupcake directions.

Punch a hole in the bottom of the yogurt container. Punch a hole in the center of the cardboard circle. Thread the yarn through the circle and knot the end. You may want to tie on a piece of twig to keep the yarn from pulling out through the hole. Thread the other end of the yarn through the hole in the bottom of the cup. Press the birdseed mixture into the cup, around the yarn, so the yarn will go right through the center of the birdseed. Pull the yarn up tight so the cardboard circle fits against the birdseed mixture. Let it harden. Tie a loop at the end of the yarn for hanging.

Peel the cup away, and the birdseed will be shaped like a bell, ready to hang from a tree so the flock can feast!

Winter Treat Garlands

Materials

Oranges

Bread: day-old is best

Heavy-duty thread and yarn needle

Knife

Tear the bread into fourths. Ask a grown-up to help you slice the oranges in rounds and then cut each round in fourths.

Thread the needle with about a yard of thread and string the food in a pattern, leaving a few inches between foods.

When you have several lengths strung, put on warm clothes and head outside to decorate a tree or bush with natural goodies for the winter birds.

This can be a fun holiday alternative to plastic and electric holiday decorations outdoors, plus the birds will love this treat.

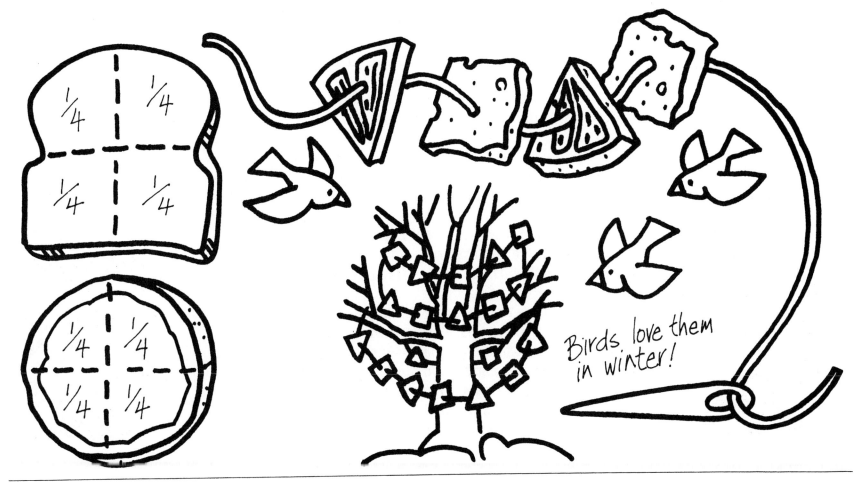

Birds love them in winter!

WREATHS

Wreaths have long been used to show honor or joy. In ancient Egypt, flowers were sewn to cloth bands tied around the head. Wreaths were given as prizes to athletes in ancient Greece (at the first Olympic Games). Warriors, poets, and great speakers (orators) also won them. In Victorian England, a guest of honor at a party might have a wreath of flowers surrounding his or her chair. Wreaths are symbols of welcome and are popular decorating items year round, now.

Making wreaths gives you a chance to use fun and unusual natural materials, like cattails, grasses, and conifers, while creating something that makes a super gift or decoration. Consider using throwaways, too. Experiment with all those collectibles you've been saving, and use them to make a one-of-a-kind wreath with a message that's totally environment-friendly.

You need a base to glue or tie things onto. Cardboard or wire can be saved to make a base. Not all wreaths are round; yours can be oval, heart-shaped, square — or even football-shaped! Let your imagination and the materials guide you.

And, wreaths don't have to just hang on a wall. Use yours to honor someone with a thank-you, as a birthday surprise, or just to say, "you are special to me."

GRAPEVINE WREATH

Materials

Grapevines, several 3' sections

Decorations you've saved: ribbons, bells, dried flowers

Scraps of wire or twine for tying

Glue

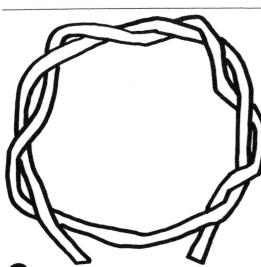

Grapevine cuttings can be obtained from gardeners doing fall pruning. Trim or pull the leaves away, leaving lengths of thin flexible vine. Take a single piece, and shape it into a circle, extending the ends so they can be wrapped over and under the rest of the circle. You may need to use thin wire or twine scraps to hold the vines in shape. Smaller wreaths are easier to form than large ones.

Keep wrapping and adding new vines, until it is the thickness you want. Tuck the ends inside the wreath, and trim away any pieces that extend unevenly.

Grapevine wreaths are wonderful as they are, but you will be tempted to decorate them with dried flowers, leaves, ribbons, or almost anything you have around. You can stick little things in between the twisted vines.

Until they are secure, use thin wire to hold items in place, or use a hot glue gun (grown-up use only).

You might turn yours into a "Get Well" wreath, with little surprises tucked in, or make a special personalized one for someone's graduation or birthday, by sticking in mementos and tiny surprises.

PINE CONE WREATH

Materials ✦✦🐦

Pine cones in various shapes and sizes

Wreath base

Glue or thin wire scraps

Pine cone wreaths are a good family project. You need a wreath base to attach the cones to. It can be any size you'd like. If you choose a wire base, you can push the cones between the wire to secure them, or attach them with short scraps of thin wire.

If you use a base made by cutting a large donut shape from sturdy cardboard (such as a pizza base), you can attach the cones with a hot glue gun (grown-up use only). Tub and tile caulk, sold in tubes, works well, too.

Splatter paint your cones a shimmering silver if you'd like or leave them natural. Arrange them in a pattern or attach haphazardly. Add other natural materials such as dried flowers and autumn leaves, or use cones only, perhaps with a festive bow. Attach a sturdy wire loop to the back of the wreath and hang.

Glue each cone to the base with a squirt of caulk.

Cut cardboard bases in a variety of wreath shapes.

Pine cones are excellent art and craft materials. They are lightweight, unbreakable, come in lots of shapes and sizes, and they're free for the gathering during a walk in the woods.

When you go searching for cones, leave behind those that haven't opened to release seeds. They may grow seedlings for the next forest, or provide seeds for squirrels and chipmunks to eat. Instead, find cones that have the tips spread open. They look much prettier in your craft projects, too.

SEED MOSAIC WREATH

Materials

Assorted dry beans and seeds

Paper plate or sturdy cardboard

Glue

Scissors

Seeds are all around you. If you walk outdoors in the fall, you will find many different kinds. Check for pods, nuts, and seeds from wild grasses and from your flower garden. Look for seeds while you are eating, too. Many fruits and vegetables can provide interesting seeds to rinse and dry for project use. Watermelon, cherries, pumpkins — all are good sources for seeds. You are really reusing what would be thrown away! And don't forget dried peas and different varieties of colorful beans.

Use the scissors to cut out the center of a paper plate to create your wreath base, or use cardboard cut into a donut-shape (or other shape) for your base. Pizza box cardboard is excellent for this project.

Spread glue on small sections of the wreath at a time and position seeds and beans to create an interesting effect or design. You can use all the same seed or different textures, sizes, shapes, and colors. You can mix them together or create very interesting patterns. Whichever you decide, the wreath will be your wonderful creation — perfect for hanging in your kitchen!

CORNHUSK WREATH

Materials ✿✿🕊

Cornhusks (save from corn on the cob or purchase)

Pan of water

Wire coat hanger and pliers

Masking tape

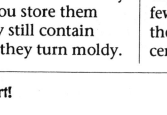usks are nature's protective jacket for the corn seeds, keeping out insects and birds that might eat the kernels before they can grow into new corn plants.

Cornhusks can be purchased in craft stores, in Mexican food sections of the grocery store, or saved when you prepare corn on the cob. If saving fresh husks, let them dry on newspaper, and then store uncovered in a box in a dry place. If you store them while they still contain moisture, they turn moldy.

Use pliers to shape the coat hanger into a round or other-shaped base for your wreath. (You may want a grown-up to help you.) Wrap the wire ends with masking tape to secure.

Wet the cornhusks as you use them, so they are easy to shape. Let them soak a bit in the pan of water, if they are very dry and brittle.

Fold the husk in half to make a loop. Lay it under the wire and pull the tail of the husk over the wire and through the loop, creating a knot. Pull securely. Knot on as many husks as will fit, completely covering the wire.

When the wire is filled with knotted husks, trim the ends of the husks to even them up. Tie on a colorful ribbon or bow made from a scrap of bright, printed fabric. You can slip thin wire around a few pine cones and fasten them to the base for accents, if you wish.

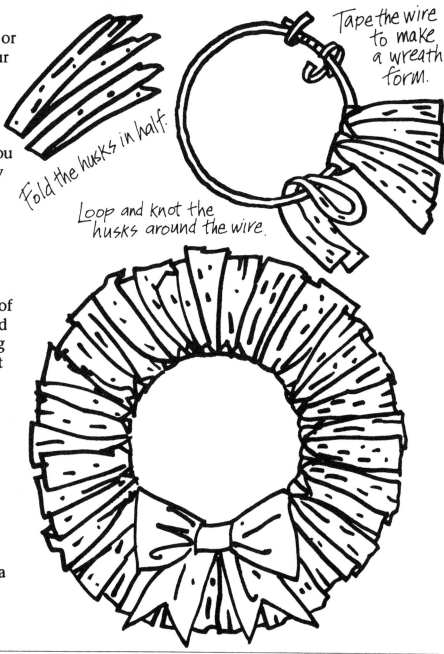

Fold the husks in half.

Tape the wire to make a wreath form.

Loop and knot the husks around the wire.

DRIED APPLE WREATH

Materials ★★★🦃

1 dozen firm, fresh apples

1 cup lemon juice

2 teaspoons salt

12" cardboard wreath shape
(use a pizza base)

Ribbon, if desired

6" wire or cord for hanging

Craft knife or scissors

Wire cake racks and cookie sheet

Towel

Adhesive: use thick, tacky-type
glue, or latex caulking

Mix the lemon juice and salt
in a bowl. Slice the apples about
1/8" thick, putting the slices in
the lemon juice mixture to prevent browning.

Drain on a towel and pat dry.
Spread the apple slices on the
wire racks and place on the
cookie sheet. Dry in the hot sun
for a few days, bringing them
indoors at night. You can also
dry them in the oven at 140° F
for 5 – 6 hours.

Trace the wreath shape around a dinner
plate; ask a grown-up to cut out the center
from the cardboard circle.

To assemble the wreath, glue the apple slices
to the cardboard wreath shape. Do the inner
and outer edges first, then overlap with a
row down the center.

Poke a hole in the cardboard and tie the
wire or cord in a loop, for hanging. If you
would like a ribbon bow, tie it first, plump-
ing it into shape, and then fasten it to the
wreath with a piece of wire.

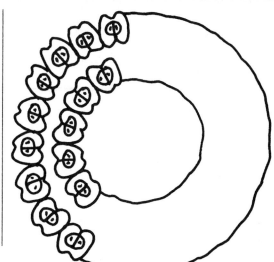

Glue apple slices
to wreath base.

Cover the base
with dry apple slices.

POPCORN WREATH

Materials ✷

Cardboard base (a pizza box is perfect)

Lots of popped corn

White glue

Yarn, or ribbon, and scissors

Ask a grown-up to cut out the center of the cardboard to create the wreath base. Punch a hole near the edge and tie a loop of yarn through it to be used for hanging later.

Pour glue out on some newspaper or a recycled meat tray. Put the popped corn into two bowls — one to eat and one to dip in glue and stick onto the wreath base!

Cover the base by dipping popcorn in glue and pressing in place. Decorate with tiny yarn or ribbon bows, glued on here and there, if you wish.

GROWING THINGS

Nature is fun to observe, but you can take an active part in helping things along. You can grow a garden, plant a tree, provide habitat for wild animals — all while enjoying yourself, using all of your senses and sensibilities, and creating with your hands.

Look around you and decide what the possibilities are. Can you grow a garden? Fill a window box? Start seeds in a flower pot or cuttings in a jar and transplant them somewhere else later? Select flowers and plants with a variety of scents, colors, and shapes. Try planting some seeds that will surprise you, like gourds. Then, you can save them and create all kinds of things. If you have never done any planting, ask a neighbor who has a pretty garden or lots of plants in the window, or ask your teacher or librarian for some help. Once you get started, you'll see there are lots of opportunities to decide what you like to plant and grow. And remember, you can grow plants whether you live in a big city or in the country, or anywhere in between!

DISH GARDEN

Materials

Used, large plastic jug

Your choice of vegetable or fruit (see next page)

Birdseed

Charcoal briquettes

Sponge

Sand and water

Trim the jug so that you have a planting bowl about 1" high on the sides. (Decorate with permanent markers, if you wish.) If you have a piece of charcoal, such as a barbecue briquette, crush it and sprinkle at the bottom of the bowl to prevent the soil from turning moldy. Fill the bowl with moist sand.

Decide which plants you want to grow, selecting from the list on the next page. Follow the directions for each selection.

After you have planted your choices, tear a sponge into medium-sized pieces.

Soak the pieces in water, and then sprinkle birdseed into the holes of the sponge pieces. Press the sponges down into the sand between your plantings. Keep the sponges moist until the birdseed sprouts. It'll be the first thing that starts to grow in your little garden. You can place some pretty shells or pebbles around the plantings. Keep the sand moist, but not too wet, and place in a sunny spot.

Plants lose water through their leaves. You will see drops form inside a terrarium cover. One acre of corn plants loses about 324,000 gallons of water in one summer. Talk about humidity!

NATURE NOTE

Soak sponge pieces in water, and dip in grass seed. Add them to your dish garden. Keep moist until seeds sprout.

The Plants:

Carrots: Carrots must be started in water, so begin them a few days before you put your garden together. Cut the carrot tops off, leaving about 1" of carrot below the top. Set the tops in a bowl of water until they begin to sprout new leaves on top.

The other plants will sprout directly in the moist sand, if you prepare them as follows:

Pineapple: Cut off the top 2" of the fruit (the part with the spiky leaves). Let it dry for 2 – 3 days, and then plant it in the moist sand.

Beets: Cut the tops off, as you did for carrots. Trim the leaves off and plant the top in the sand.

Grapefruit: Soak the seeds overnight, before planting in the moist sand. (Grapefruit shells, filled with potting soil, make interesting pots for the plants themselves.)

Potato: Cut into sections, each with an eye or two, and plant.

FOREST TERRARIUM

Materials ★★★🦆

Two 2-liter soda pop bottles

Pebbles

Sand

Soil

Charcoal briquettes

Mosses, ferns, or small green plants

If you live where it's possible and can obtain the owner's permission, take a hike in a wooded area and gather a few tiny plants, such as moss from the side of tree trunks or rocks, and tiny ferns. Of course, you'll take only what you will use. As you know, never take the whole plant, but just a bit from a large clump, and be sure to re-cover the roots of the plant you have disturbed with soil.

When gathering, use a teaspoon to dig lightly and carefully around the roots. Lift them gently, leaving soil surrounding the roots. Take along some old newspapers to dampen and wrap around the plants to keep them moist and a small, cardboard box to lay your specimens in, as they are very delicate. Don't crowd them, and don't let the plants dry out. You will need to plant them immediately.

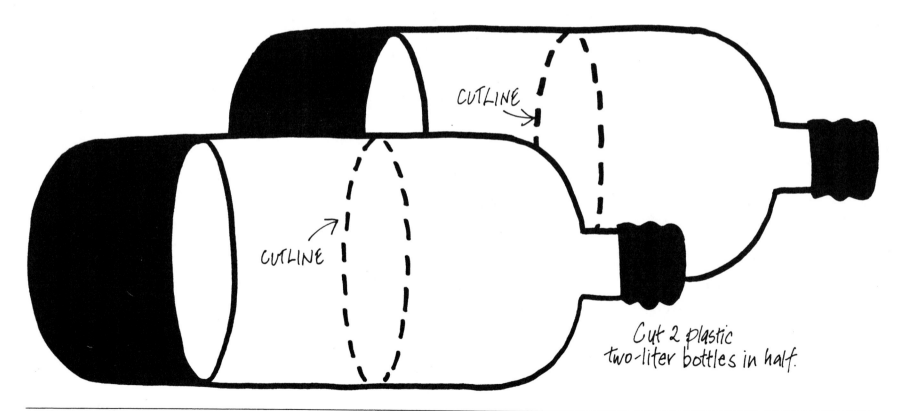

CUTLINE

CUTLINE

Cut 2 plastic two-liter bottles in half.

If you can't take a walk in the woods, look around for plant sources. You can take "cuttings" from established houseplants. Plants like philodendron and ivy are easy to grow from cuttings. Use a table knife or scissors to snip off a 6" piece at the end of a stem. Set it in a glass half-full of water until roots begin to appear. Then, it can be planted in a pot, or your terrarium. Share cuttings from your plants with friends, and create new plants from "old."

Plant in one bottom half.

Pull the dark section out of the other bottom half and use it as a cover.

Slide the cover over the garden.

You can make a beautiful forest terrarium by recycling two clear plastic 2-liter soda pop bottles. Get grown-up help to cut them both in half, using a sharp knife. Pull out the dark bottom in the base of one, so that it is clear. Use the other for planting.

To set up the terrarium, first put pebbles in the bottom for drainage, then a layer of sand and crushed charcoal briquettes. Spread 1" – 2" of soil over the top.

Create a little forest scene by arranging ferns, mosses, and small green plants. Interesting rocks and branches add more realism. Water very lightly. The moisture inside the terrarium will help keep the plants moist.

When your terrarium looks the way you want it to, slip the clear bottle half over the planter for a lid. Your terrarium should be placed by a window, but not where the sun will shine directly on it or the plants will dry out. Water it now and then. If water drops appear on the sides of the terrarium, open it for a few hours to remove the extra moisture.

POTATO PORCUPINE

Materials ✹

Large potato

Twigs or toothpicks

Eyes: two whole cloves

Grass seed

Soil

Spoon

Use the spoon to dig and hollow out one side of the potato. Fill the hollow with a little soil and sprinkle grass seed in it. Stick twigs or toothpicks in for legs. Position the cloves for eyes.

Keep moist and in a few days you will see the porcupine sprout its quills! In about two weeks, it will look really fluffy.

Try creating some other kinds of "furry" creatures, perhaps using more than one potato, twigs, and unusual plantings.

Use a spoon to hollow out the potato.

Plant grass seed. Decorate with clove eyes and twig legs.

"If you want to be happy for a year, plant a garden. If you want to be happy for a lifetime, plant a tree." *Unknown*

NATURE NOTE

EGGHEADS

Materials ✳

Eggshells and egg carton

Soil

Grass seed

Permanent marking pens or paint

Rinse and save eggshells in an egg carton for awhile, so you have several to work with. The best eggshells for this project are those broken straight across, slightly larger than half a shell.

To make an egghead, first select a large half shell. Draw on comical facial features with permanent marking pen or paint (or use both).

Fill the shell with some soil, sprinkle grass seed in it, and moisten with water. Set several eggheads in the egg carton near a sunny window, and in about a week, they will have a funny head of hair. You can trim the "hair" with scissors and watch it grow back again! When you are finished enjoying your smiling creations, plant the entire egghead in your garden; the shell will provide minerals for the soil as it decays.

Save eggshells. Fill with soil and grass seed, then decorate with pens or paint. Wait for your Egghead to sprout hair.

GLORIOUS GOURDS

Gourds appear in an amazing variety of shapes, colors, and textures. Fresh gourds look nice in centerpieces. Dried gourds can be cut, sanded, drilled, and wood-burned into clever and interesting objects.

Growing your own gourds is fun. They need a warm, sunny spot, with room to stretch out (or up). If you don't have garden space, you can purchase them fresh in grocery stores and garden markets, usually during the fall and winter.

If you are going to leave the gourds as they are for decoration, give them a shiny finish with a coat of acrylic floor wax or rub on some car wax. If you are going to make craft items from the gourds, don't a wax them.

There are rain forests in Alaska, California, and Washington. They are called wet conifer rain forests.

Choose a gourd that has a tear-drop shape. Use the nail to poke a hole through the top. Straighten the coat hanger and push it through the gourd. Use the pliers to twist the wire into a loop for hanging.

Using the paring knife and spoon, carefully hollow out a rounded hole about 2" across, for the bird to enter. You may want to ask for some grown-up help to puncture the gourd's tough outer skin. Shake out the seeds that have dried inside the gourd.

To make a perch for the birds, work a hole into the gourd below the opening and push the stick in through it.

Hang from a tree branch and wait for your new feathered neighbor to move in!

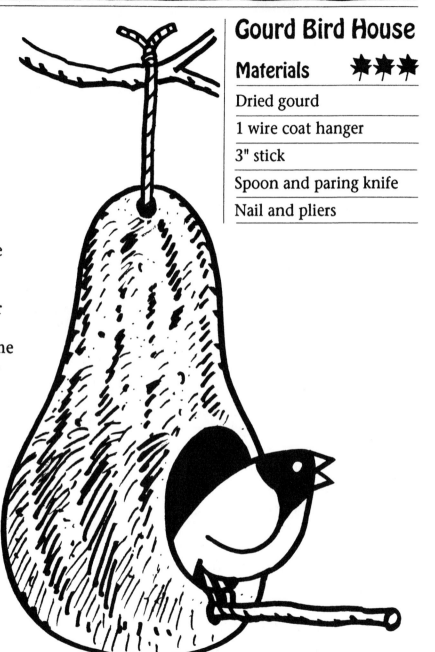

Gourd Bird House

Materials ✹ ✹ ✹

Dried gourd
1 wire coat hanger
3" stick
Spoon and paring knife
Nail and pliers

Gourd Bowl

Materials ★★★

Dried gourd

Sandpaper

Small hand saw

Spoon

Choose a gourd that's round in shape or has a rounded end that will make a good bowl shape. Ask a grown-up to help you saw an opening across the gourd. (You can cut it either vertically or horizontally, depending on how your gourd is shaped and what will give it the best balanced base.)

Scrape out the contents with a spoon, saving the seeds for another project such as the seed mosaic (see page 69). Scrape it clean and smooth the cut edges with sandpaper.

The outside can be decorated with paint, marking pens, or designs made with a wood-burning pen. Coat with acrylic finish, if you want a shiny look.

Useful items that Native American Indians made from dried gourds many, many years ago are on display in museums; your gourd bowl will last a long time if stored in a dry place. Fill it with dried flowers or leaves, for a truly natural piece of art!

Cut a gourd in half to make a bowl.

CRYSTAL ROCK CANDY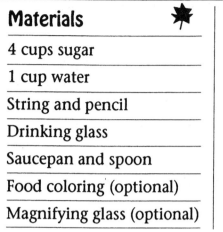

Minerals form crystals when the atoms have room to grow freely, while the mineral is being formed. Some crystals are so rare and hard that they are used in jewelry. We call them gemstones. Diamonds, emeralds, sapphire, and rubies are good examples. Some common crystals are salt, sugar, ice, and quartz rock.

Not all crystals are edible, nor are most works of art, but these crystal works of art are old-time favorite candies that kids used to buy for a treat at the general store!

Materials

4 cups sugar

1 cup water

String and pencil

Drinking glass

Saucepan and spoon

Food coloring (optional)

Magnifying glass (optional)

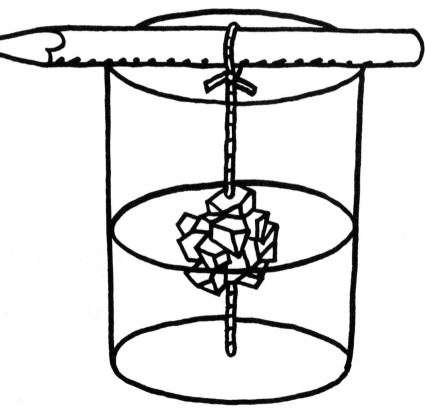

Ask a grown-up to help you heat 2 cups of sugar and the water in a saucepan. Stir until the sugar dissolves. Add 2 more cups sugar and continue heating and stirring until clear.

Carefully pour the solution into a drinking glass. Tie a length of string from the pencil so the string hangs in the solution. Crystals will form on the string within a few hours. Examine the crystals with a magnifying lens and touch them with your fingertips and tongue. What do you discover?

Try several different strings in one glass of sugar solution. Add food coloring to create colorful crystals. Create crystal sculptures you can taste!

PRINTING

Making prints is a fun way to give life to discarded or reusable materials. Two things determine the nature of your print: your choice of brayer or tool to apply the ink with and your choice of material to print on. For printing, select from old sponges, stale bread, half a potato or orange, fallen leaves, empty thread spools, discarded nuts, bolts, or paper clips — whatever you can find!

Next, select a material to print on: paper grocery bags, tissue paper you have saved (ask a grown-up for help with pressing it smooth with a warm steam iron), cardboard and packaging materials, scrap paper, homemade paper (see page 18) — all provide good surfaces to print designs on.

You can also use old T-shirts, handkerchiefs, fabric scraps, pillow cases, and cut-up sheets (for making great personal flags to hang in your room and bandannas). Use acrylic or fabric paints for fabric printing.

You can use your printed materials to make gift bags, book covers, note cards, gift wrap, place mats, or artwork to frame. Your imagination plus the materials you gather will give new life to discarded items.

Spider Web Prints

Spiders eat insects that they catch in the sticky webs they build. Webs differ, depending upon the type of spider that makes them. A house spider creates a few strands that go in any direction, while some spiders make webs in sheets, and others create web funnels to trap insects. Some orb spiders create delicate works of art attached to stalks of grass.

It takes about an hour for a spider to build a web, usually at night. Look for one in the morning when the slant of the sun makes them easier to find. Look under fences, in grassy areas, or next to the base of buildings.

Don't disturb a web where a spider is working or where a fly has been caught. That might be a spider's breakfast! Instead, look for webs that have been deserted, and recycle that web into art!

Materials

Spray paint or non-aerosol hairspray

Lightweight cardboard or stiff tag board — a piece about 6" x 6"

If you are using black spray paint, choose white cardboard. If using hairspray, choose black cardboard, or paint your cardboard a bright color. The contrast helps the web show up better.

Gently spray the deserted web from both sides, and then hold the cardboard behind the web. Pinch off the web's guide lines (where it is fastened to the grass or fence), so that now the web is resting on the cardboard. The wet hairspray will act like a glue, fastening it to the cardboard as it dries. Isn't it a beautiful, intricate design? Aren't you amazed that a tiny spider can quickly create such a beautiful work of art? This is nature at its artistic best! Why not weave or braid some grass to make a frame for your spider web art.

Find an old, deserted spider web.

Spray with hairspray, so it will stick to a piece of cardboard. Braid some grass for a frame.

Incredible Food Printing

Almost any type of natural foodstuff can be used to make great prints. Potatoes are commonly used, but have you tried using nutshells, orange slices, uncooked macaroni shapes, or rolling corn on the cob in paint and printing with it? Search the pantry, then pull out the paints and newspapers and try food printing — buffet-style!

This type of printing is fun to do, and turns paper bags you have saved into gift wrap, book covers, or decorative shopping bags.

Lay out newspapers to protect your work surface. Prepare the foods by cutting or slicing, vertically or horizontally, or cutting the foods into shapes. (Cut apples horizontally to get a star shape in the center, and slice oranges horizontally to see the natural design of sections.)

Pour paint onto trays. Dip the foods and then press them in place on the printing paper. Experiment by using different patterns and colors, as well as different textures and colors of paper to print on.

You can give new life to old T-shirts, caps, pillowcases, sheets, or aprons, by printing fun designs on them. To print on fabric, use acrylic or fabric paints.

Materials

- Fresh vegetables and fruits
- Newspapers
- Paint: tempera dries brightest
- Paper to print on
- Trays, plates, or recycled materials to hold paint

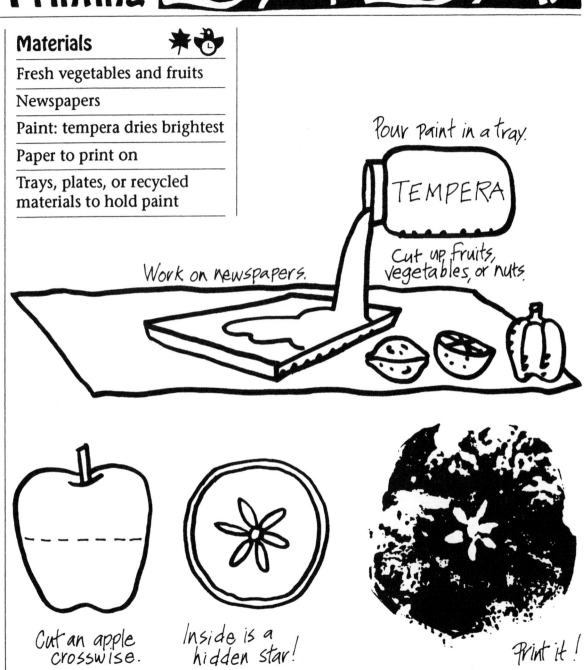

Pour paint in a tray.

Work on newspapers.

Cut up fruits, vegetables, or nuts.

TEMPERA

Cut an apple crosswise.

Inside is a hidden star!

Print it!

Mushroom Spore Prints

Materials

Fresh mushroom: use one with a flat cap that hasn't opened yet

Colored paper

Glass jar

Gently pull the stem away from the mushroom cap. Place the cap on a piece of colored paper, and cover with a glass jar. Leave it alone for about four hours. The mushroom cap will open, and the spores will drop onto the paper.

Try spore prints on different colors of paper, looking for interesting contrasts. Some spores are dark, some light.

To preserve your print and keep it from smearing, spray lightly with extra-hold hair spray in a non-aerosol pump can. Spore prints done on colorful pieces of paper make very attractive stationery.

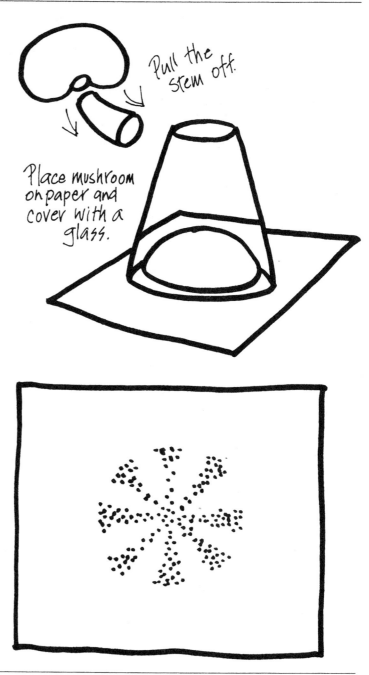

Pull the stem off.

Place mushroom on paper and cover with a glass.

Spores will drop onto the paper in an interesting pattern.

FAST FACT

A mushroom isn't really a plant. It's a fungi, which means it grows from spores, not seeds.

Tin Can Printing

Materials ★ ★ 🕙

Tin can

Yarn or heavy string and scissors

White glue in a small bowl

Tempera paints

Paper to print on

Newspapers

Packaging tray you have saved

Use the newspapers to protect your table top.

Remove both ends from the can. Pour some glue in the bowl. Cut a length of yarn about 12" long. Dip it in the glue and then wrap the yarn around the can, creating a pattern or design with the yarn. Add more lengths of yarn as needed. Let the glue dry completely.

Pour some paint on the tray. Roll the can in it, and then roll the can over the paper, pressing firmly to print. If you want to use several colors of paint at once, brush the paint onto the can in sections, then roll on the paper to print.

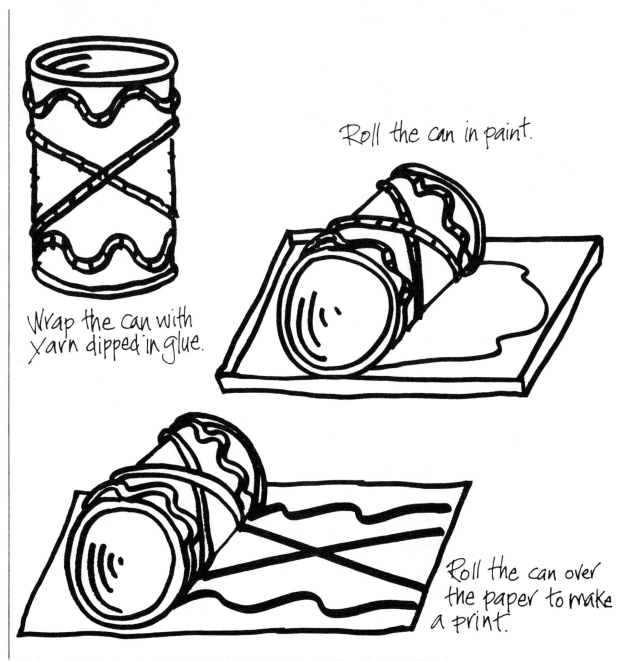

Wrap the can with yarn dipped in glue.

Roll the can in paint.

Roll the can over the paper to make a print.

WEEDS, HERBS, & OTHER GREAT STUFF

No matter where you live, you can take a "walk on the wild side"! You can find plants, animals, and nature in its wildest form all around you. Can you find a weed growing in a crack in the sidewalk? Close your eyes and smell it's fragrance, then brush it gently against your cheek. Enjoy even the tiniest bit of nature around you. Whether in the city or in the country, nature is there if you open your eyes and mind to it. Did you notice the wasp's nest under the eave, the spider's web at the mailbox, the moss stuck between the bricks? You don't have to wander far to find wild things, because they are living right next to you.

Notice how many different kinds of plants are growing in just a small section of ground. Look at them from the ground up. Tiny plants may be hugging the ground, others surrounding them above. Look along walls and up in the trees, too. Close your eyes and sniff the different plants you find. Can you identify them without looking? Depending upon the time of year, you may find plants ready to send out seeds from pods. Blow or shake them, and watch the tiny seeds disperse into the air, to start next year's plants. And so nature's wondrous cycle continues.

TREAT NATURE WITH CARE

There are a few important things to consider, before helping yourself to any plants. Of course, you'll be polite and ask for permission, if you are on private property. You won't pick flowers in public gardens in parks — they are for everyone to enjoy. If the flowers you want to use are wildflowers, leave plenty of blossoms to turn to seed so the plants can reseed themselves. Never pull plants up by the root; instead, cut them with scissors, so plants that grow from the root mass can regenerate themselves.

There is plenty available free for the taking — autumn leaves, sprigs of different kinds of grasses, a tiny clump of moss, cattails, pine cones, pebbles, shells, and fallen bark.

Also, be careful that you aren't collecting in an area that has been recently sprayed with harmful chemicals that can contaminate your hands and your projects.

Take a paper sack and an empty box to carry your nature treasures in. You will also need a pair of blunt-ended scissors to clip stems, and some old string to tie small bundles of plants together. Plan your projects before going, so that you only collect the materials you will use, and you won't be wasting anything.

Flowers: Pressed & Dried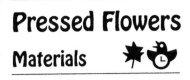

Pressed Flowers

Materials

Old newspapers

Flowers

Scissors

Is there a vacant lot near your home where purple violets or pink hepatica grow wild? Did you plant a box of pansies or violas this spring? If so, these are perfect for pressing.

Carefully collect a few flowers by snipping them on long stems, keeping all the leaves on them. Only pick as many as you need, and never too many from one plant.

Now, spread the flowers out on the newspapers, pressing with your fingers to flatten and shape them a bit. Cover the flowers with a few sheets of newspaper, stacking the flower-filled pages on top of each other. Press down with heavy books. Wait about a week before taking the pressed flowers out; store them in shoe boxes. You can make several projects with pressed flowers, so make up an ample supply to use another time. You can also dry leaves of different shapes and sizes.

Stack heavy books on top.

Cover with layers of newspapers.

Position flowers on newspapers.

Dried Flowers

Materials ✳

1 cup borax
(purchase in a supermarket)

2 cups cornmeal

Shoe box

Another way to preserve flowers is by drying them. Pressed flowers are flattened, while dried flowers are three-dimensional and can be arranged in a vase or basket, as if they were still alive. Roses, strawflowers, and purple statice all dry very well. Maybe you can plant some or ask a neighbor if you can pick a few flowers. Sometimes, a florist will let you have some old flowers to use for pressing and drying.

Mix the borax and cornmeal to make a drying agent. Spread some in the shoe box. Gently lay the flowers on the mixture. Carefully cover the flowers completely with the mixture. Put the lid on the box, and put it away in a closet for about a month. (Mark on your calendar when the flowers will be ready.)

Cover the flowers completely; then put on the lid.

Mini-Vase & Flowers

Materials ✳

Thread spool (remove the labels; paint if you wish)

Tiny dried flowers or weeds

6" of narrow ribbon or yarn

This makes a simple, country-style gift for Mother's Day, May Day, or as party favors. A grouping of three of these looks very pretty on a bureau or mantel.

Break the flower stems off if they are too long, so they set nicely in the hole in the spool. Dip the stem ends in a little glue, and arrange them inside the hole of the spool.

Wrap the ribbon around the spool, and tie in a bow. Secure the bow with a dot of glue. Trim the ends evenly.

Pressed Flower Bookmarks

Materials ✹✹

Homemade paper (see page 18) or tagboard the size you want your bookmark to be.

Pressed flowers or leaves

Small scrap of nylon net, tulle, or organdy fabric

Narrow ribbon or flat lace trim

Glue that dries clear

Here's a nice gift project using dried, pressed flowers. While you work on this, think of how pretty the flowers looked in the field or garden. That will help you arrange them in a very natural way.

Cut the paper and net the size you want to make your bookmark. Gently position the dried flowers on top of the paper. Use a few dots of glue to hold them in position. Using a tiny amount of glue around the edges, glue the net on top of the flowers. Position the ribbon or lace around the edges and glue in place.

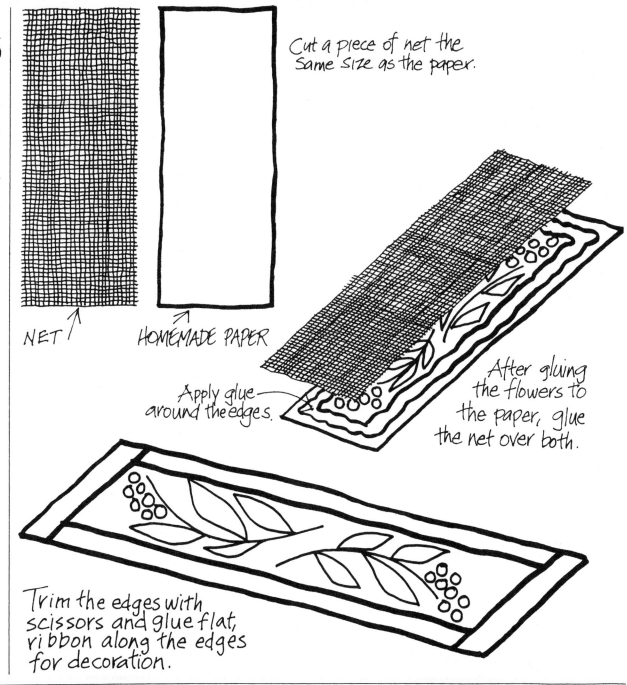

NET ↑   HOMEMADE PAPER ↑

Cut a piece of net the same size as the paper.

Apply glue around the edges.

After gluing the flowers to the paper, glue the net over both.

Trim the edges with scissors and glue flat, ribbon along the edges for decoration.

Potpourri

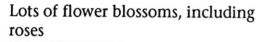

Materials

Lots of flower blossoms, including roses

1 tablespoon mixed spices (cloves, cinnamon, nutmeg, mace, or allspice) and/or 1 tablespoon dry, mixed herbs

Few drops potpourri oil (optional)

Small, airtight containers

Ribbon

Pans for drying

"Art is like a border of flowers along the course of civilization."
Lincoln Steffens

ART SPEAK

What's one of the most wonderful things about outdoors? It smells so fresh and sweet — that is, if we take care of the air around us. Well, you can capture some of that outdoor goodness and bring it inside. You can make potpourri (poe-pour-REE) from just about any dried plant material that has a pleasant scent.

One way to obtain fresh flowers to use, if you don't have them in a garden, is to contact a florist shop, and ask for the flowers that have to be discarded. You may end up with lots of sweet-smelling roses, gardenias, and carnations for free.

To make the potpourri, gather lots of flower blossoms. Try to find different colors and scents. Roses are the most popular and should make up most of your mixture.

Now, pull apart the flower blossoms, discarding all but the petals. Place the petals in pans to dry, away from sunlight. Mix them a few times a day. When completely dry, sprinkle with a spoonful of mixed spices or dried herbs (rosemary, marjoram, cedar needles, mint, sage, or thyme). A few drops of potpourri oil (available at craft stores) can also be sprinkled on to intensify the scent.

Mix the dry petals with your hands and scoop them into clean, airtight containers. Baby food jars are perfect. Paint the lids and tie a ribbon around the jar to make a special gift.

To use potpourri, keep the lid closed until you want to scent a room; then, open the lid for a while. To maintain the nice scent, add drops of potpourri oil.

Potpourri Sachet

Materials

Dried potpourri mixture
(see page 92)

6" square of nylon netting,
or lightweight, cotton,
print fabric

Rubber band

6" length of satin ribbon

Want to make a special gift for
your sister or aunt, grandmother
or neighbor? Here's a simple way
to make a sachet to scent a bureau
or desk drawer. These are also pretty
hung from the tree as Christmas
ornaments when made with red and
green fabric squares.

Lay the fabric square on a table top
and spoon about two tablespoons of
the dried potpourri into the center.
Bring the edges of the fabric to the
center and secure with a rubber
band. Then tie a pretty bow at the
center with the satin ribbon.

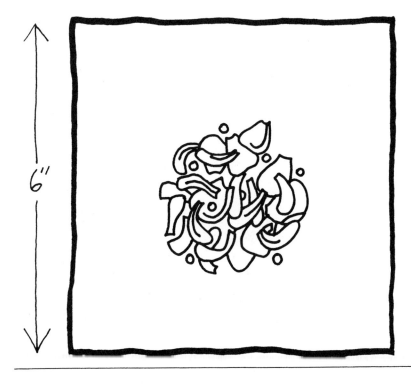

6"

Solar Art

Materials

Weeds, leaves, berries, flowers — whatever you have gathered

Studio proof paper and fixer (buy at a photography supply store)

Water

2 dishpans or square cake pans

Here's a way to use your environment to "capture" nature's beauty! This is a special kind of photography that uses the light from the sun to create shadow pictures. Select weeds and leaves with different shapes and feathery edges.

On a sunny day, arrange an assortment of your interesting weeds, thistles, and berries on a piece of studio proof paper and put it in bright sunlight. The plants will block the sun's rays, causing the paper under them to remain light colored, while the exposed paper turns a dark purple. It will only take a few minutes. (Lift the edge of a leaf carefully to see if it is "done.")

Ask a grown-up to prepare the fixer (it's poisonous) in one of the pans. Fill the other pan with water. Remove the plants and set the paper in the pan of fixer for five minutes. This will prevent the paper from turning completely dark in daylight. Take it out of the fixer bath, and set the paper in the pan of water for ten minutes.

You can soak more than one paper in the pans at once.

When the prints are done, lay them on newspapers to dry. If the print paper curls, stack a heavy book on it to flatten it. Your nature prints will look nice when matted or framed, and hung on the wall. You can also trim and glue the prints to folded construction paper to make greeting cards.

Arrange weeds on proof paper. Set in bright sunshine.

Soak paper in fixer for 5 minutes.

Soak paper in water for 10 minutes.

Rubbings

Materials

Leaves of different shapes and sizes

Paper

Crayons (see page 30 to make your own), colored chalks, or soft lead pencils

Newspapers

Isn't it fun to walk in the leaves, picking up different shapes and sizes that have fallen to the ground? Find a safe place to lie down on the ground and look up through the trees to the sky. Wow! Those trees are so very tall, and yet, the leaves float so slowly to the ground.

Collect several different types and sizes of leaves. Place some leaves on several layers of newspaper and position your rubbing paper over the leaves. Use the sides of the crayons to rub over the paper with steady, firm strokes, and the leaf shapes will be outlined on the paper. Try crayons, chalks, or pencil, or combinations of the three, for different effects.

Add other interesting textural items: coins, pieces of fabric and lace, paper doilies, cutouts from thin tag board, small washers, and pieces of sewing trims.

Take your crayons and paper outdoors to collect more textures. Hold the paper against different types of trees and make rubbings of the bark. Make rubbings of stucco walls, concrete sidewalks, asphalt streets, bricks. Manhole covers, tombstones, and old signs are also interesting.

Rose Petal Beads

In the past, rose petal beads were cherished remembrances of the blossoms in a grandmother's garden or a bride's bouquet. Here is a quick and easy way to make beads from the petals in your own garden or from discarded roses at the florist shop.

Materials

2/3 cup flour

2 tablespoons salt

1/3 cup water

6 cups of rose petals (pick them in the morning for best fragrance)

Large bowl and spoon

Toothpicks

Needle and thread

Mix the flour, salt, and water. Knead until smooth.

Tear the rose petals into tiny pieces. Crumble and crush them as you work to soften them and release their fragrance.

Mix the shredded petals into the dough, keeping it soft and pliable. Roll bits of dough into beads. Push toothpicks into the beads to make holes for stringing later. Set aside a few days for drying. Then, string the beads with a needle and double-knotted thread. Tie the ends of the thread together and wear as a fragrant, special necklace.

Add torn rose petals to the dough.

String with a needle and thread when dry.

Pomander

The first pomanders were made from gold or silver. They were shaped like balls and hung by a cord from the waist. They were filled with sweet-smelling herbs and spices, and used as perfumes. They were also thought to keep one from getting sick. Today, pomanders are made from fresh fruits and are hung in a closet to scent clothes and keep moths away.

Japanese floral art is called *ikebana*. It uses three main branches in an arrangement.

ART SPEAK

Materials

Firm, fresh oranges or lemons

Whole dried cloves

Toothpick or thumbtack with large plastic head

Nylon net

Ribbon or pretty yarn

Use a thumbtack with a large plastic head or a toothpick to poke holes in the orange skin, inserting a whole clove into each hole. You can randomly place the cloves in the orange, as close together as you can, or you can make a very neat vertical or horizontal pattern. If you want to add a richer, spicier scent, roll the finished pomander in a mixture of cinnamon, allspice, and nutmeg.

Now, set the pomander aside to dry for several weeks. It will shrink and get hard (as the orange gets dehydrated). Wrap it in a square of nylon net and tie the ends with the ribbon. It's ready to hang in a closet or kitchen, or give as a gift.

Poke holes with a thumbtack. Push the cloves into the holes.

Wrap the dry pomander in nylon and tie with a ribbon.

Hooray for Herbs!

Herbs are aromatic plants used for cooking, medicine, household uses, and pest control. Some common herbs are the leaves of fragrant plants like mint, rosemary, and thyme.

Spices are similar to herbs except that they are usually made from tropical plants such as cinnamon, cloves, ginger, and pepper.

You can collect wild herbs, or you can easily grow your own — in a small garden, in flower pots, or window boxes. Just be sure to give them plenty of light and water them as needed. Herb seeds can be purchased anywhere garden supplies are sold.

When picking herbs from the wilds or your garden, use scissors to snip off only the leaves you will need, leaving the roots and some leaves for continued plant growth. Most herbs grow back after several cuttings.

When gathering fresh herbs, collect more than you think you need, as they will shrink while drying. Collect on a dry morning, and then dry the herbs further on newspapers, away from light. Once completely dry, separate the leaves from the stems. Crush the leaves and store in an airtight container until you're ready to use them.

If you are working on a project and run short of your dried herbs, mix in some uncooked rice to add bulk and to stretch your herb mixture.

Herb Vinegar

Materials

Fresh or dried herbs: fennel, sage, rosemary, garlic, tarragon, or chives

Vinegar (cider, white, or balsamic)

Glass bottle with cork or nonmetal cap

Use several sprigs of fresh herbs or about 1/2 to 1 cup of loose herbs to make 1 quart of herb vinegar. You can use more or less, depending upon how strongly flavored you want the vinegar to be.

Fill the clean bottle with herbs, gently arranging the sprigs. Then, fill the bottle with vinegar. Cap or cork, and let it sit for two weeks. Tie a pretty bow around the bottle for a perfect gift.

Here's a wonderful way to reuse old bottles and savor the flavor of fresh herbs in your salads all winter long. If the labels don't peel off easily, soak the bottles in warm water for a few minutes, then scrub off. Wash them thoroughly in hot, soapy water and air dry completely.

Sweet Dreams Pillow

Materials

1 cup dried flower petals

1/2 cup dried mint

1 tablespoon crushed cloves

2 pieces of closely woven fabric, about 6" x 6" (Use broadcloth or gingham — cloth handkerchiefs are pretty, too.)

Needle, thread, and scissors

Ribbon or lace for trim (optional)

Large bowl

This pillow is for those nights when you just can't get to sleep. Place it inside your pillowcase. The scent of the herbs is said to have a relaxing effect.

Gently mix the herbs and petals in the bowl. With right sides of the fabric facing each other (so it looks inside out), sew the pillow together around the edges, leaving one side open for turning and filling. Clip the corners of the seam allowances. Turn right side out and fill gently with the dried herbs. Sew the opening closed.

You can decorate the pillow by gluing or sewing on lace or ribbon trims.

Mix herbs and dry petals.

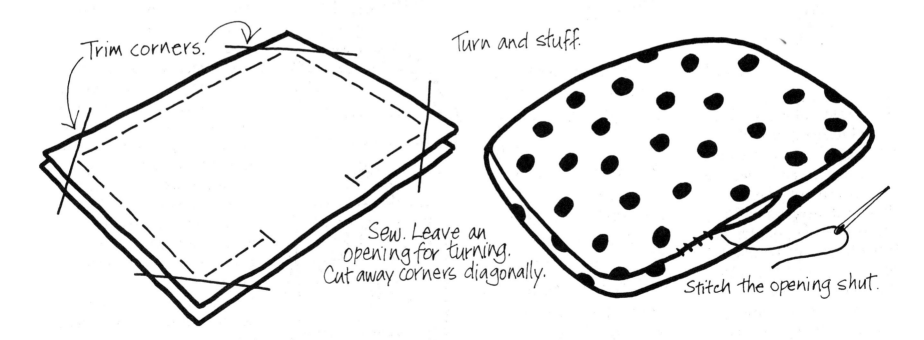

Trim corners.

Sew. Leave an opening for turning. Cut away corners diagonally.

Turn and stuff.

Stitch the opening shut.

Weed Casting

Materials ✹🐦

Weeds, flowers, leaves

Modeling clay

Plaster of Paris and utensils

Empty box, like a shoe box

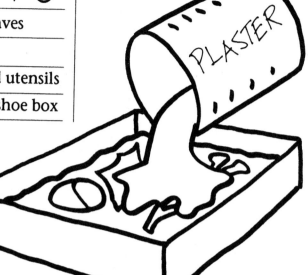

Press modeling clay into a box. Press the weeds into the clay, then remove them. Pour plaster into the box to cover the clay.

modeling clay in the shoe box bottom, up to about half an inch thick. Arrange your weeds in a pleasing pattern on top of the clay. With your fingers, gently press the weeds down into the clay and then pull them out. Their imprints will remain. If you want to change your design, smooth the clay surface and press the weeds again. Once you have your final imprint, mix the plaster in the container, following the directions on the plaster box. Pour it over the clay until the plaster is about 2" thick.

Let the plaster harden and dry; overnight is best. Then, gently tear away the sides of the box, separating the clay from the plaster casting.

Paint or stain the plaster casting, if you wish. Dark shoe polish can also be gently rubbed onto the plaster surface with a soft rag. If you want a shiny finish, brush on a coat of acrylic finish or acrylic floor wax.

If working indoors, it's a good idea to spread old newspapers to cover your work area. Be sure that you don't wash any plaster down the sink drain. To discard leftover plaster, let it harden in the container, break it up, and add it to the compost heap.

To create an interesting sculpture, first press the

To make a cast that can be hung on the wall, tie a loop of old yarn or cord. Lay it on the wet plaster and push it down so it is covered by some wet plaster. 2 or 3" of yarn must be stuck within the plaster. When hard, hang by the yarn loop.

Peannt People

Materials ✹✹

Peanuts in the shell

Fine-tip felt markers

Glue and scissors

Bits of stuffing, feathers, sequins, scraps of fabric or leather

Glue the nutty people to driftwood or stone.

Poke holes with a nail and insert twig arms and legs.

Decorate broken shells for finger puppets.

Peanuts make nutty characters! Select the size and shape of nut you want for your person — some make wonderful babies, some tall and spindly characters, and others chubby and round folk.

Draw on a face and clothing details with the markers. Add scraps of cloth for hats, robes, scarves, or capes. Glue on pieces of embroidery thread or feathers for hair. Use bits of pillow stuffing or cotton balls for beards.

You can make clever family groupings by gluing several nuts of different sizes to a piece of bark or driftwood. This looks great on a desk or bookcase. Send a peanut family to work with your mom or dad!

Use a nail to poke holes in the nut shell's body for arms and legs made of twigs or pipe cleaners. Use tacky-type glue to hold them.

Finger puppets can be made from peanut shells, too, and . . . you get to eat the nut! All you need are peanuts and a fine-tip marking pen. Break the shell across, try to get one that is long. Draw on facial features, gluing details from scraps. Put it on your finger, and bring your puppet to life!

Pine Cone Owl Sculpture

Materials ✳

Small pine cones

Felt scraps

Glue and scissors

Small branch

Tin can with pebbles or soil

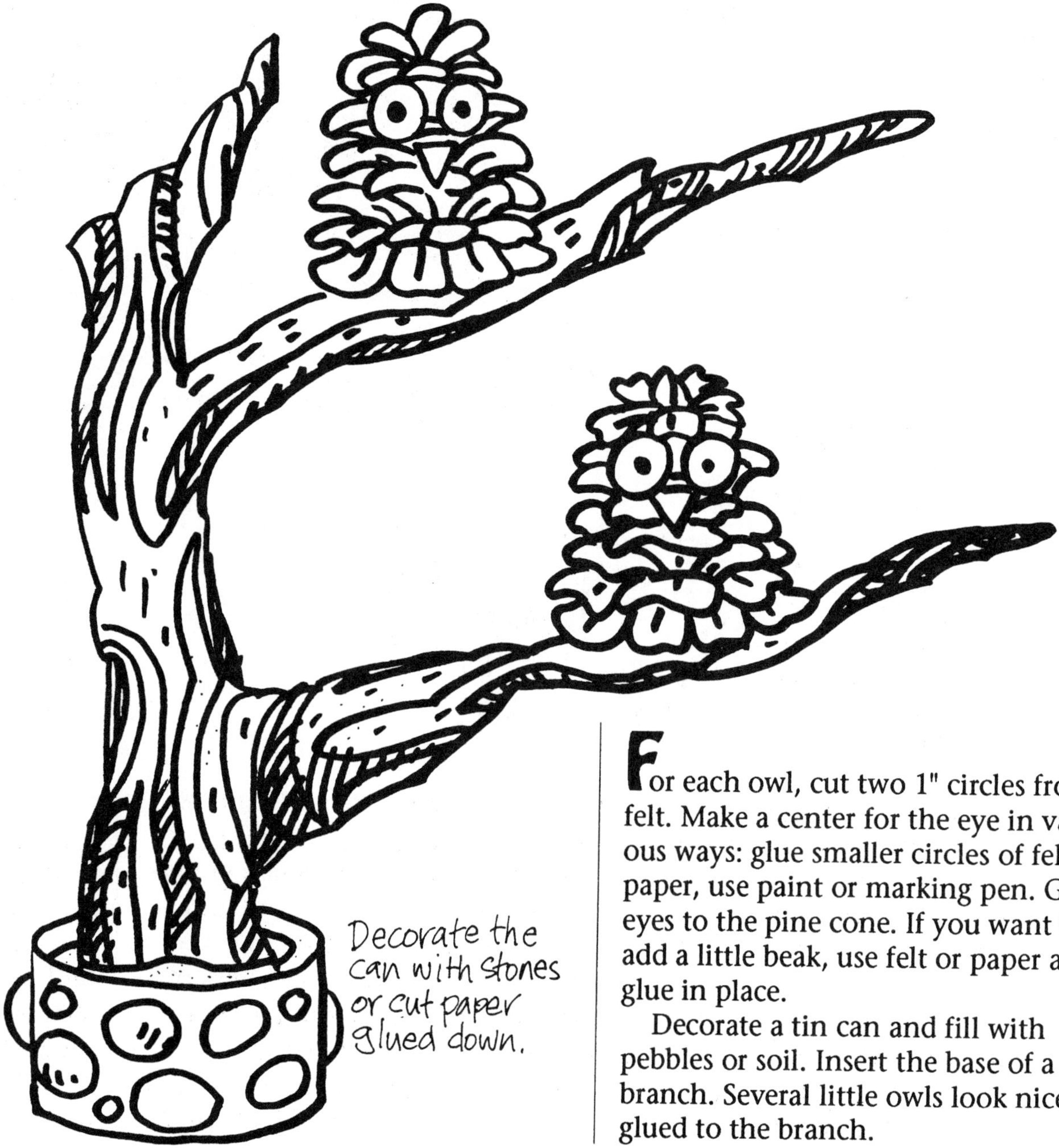

Decorate the can with stones or cut paper glued down.

For each owl, cut two 1" circles from felt. Make a center for the eye in various ways: glue smaller circles of felt or paper, use paint or marking pen. Glue eyes to the pine cone. If you want to add a little beak, use felt or paper and glue in place.

Decorate a tin can and fill with pebbles or soil. Insert the base of a branch. Several little owls look nice glued to the branch.

Weather Wonders

Have you noticed how much the weather affects you? It can change your plans for the day and your mood as well. It affects the kind of homes we live in, the type of clothing we wear, and the food we eat. It affects the plant and animal world, too. Many animals grow thick fur or go into hibernation when it's cold. Plants also have a period of inactivity during cold weather. Even fish live differently when the weather changes. Plants and animals are continually **adapting** themselves to the weather around them.

After the rain, watch to see if a rainbow appears. What colors do you see? What shape is the rainbow. Watch for rainbows in water spraying from hoses, and in crystals, too. Are the colors always in the same order?

ART SPEAK

Rainy Day Drip Paintings

Materials

Butcher paper

Powdered tempera, several colors

Shaker dispensers for the paint (Old salt shakers or spice containers work very well. You will need one for each color of powdered paint.)

When the weather forecast is "light rain on the way," prepare for a rain painting. Work outside before the rain begins. Spread out a large sheet of paper, using stones or something heavy to weight down the paper's edges.

Fill the shaker dispensers with powdered paint. Sprinkle the powdered tempera randomly over the paper. As it rains, the raindrops will mix and blend the paint colors. After a few minutes, go out and discover what designs the rain has made for you. Bring in the wet painting and let dry on layers of old newspapers. You have a real "watercolor," created by a very famous artist — nature, herself!

Another way to do a rain painting, is to leave the paper outside to be-come wet. Once the drizzling stops, go outside with the shakers and sprinkle a design on the wet paper. Carefully, carry it inside to dry on newspaper. Which kind of rain painting do you like best?

Snow Painting

Materials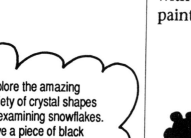

Paint: tempera, food coloring, or natural dyes

Colored chalk

Large brushes or old spray bottles

Cans or jugs to hold paint

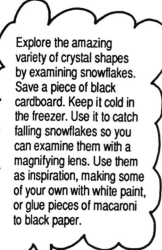

Explore the amazing variety of crystal shapes by examining snowflakes. Save a piece of black cardboard. Keep it cold in the freezer. Use it to catch falling snowflakes so you can examine them with a magnifying lens. Use them as inspiration, making some of your own with white paint, or glue pieces of macaroni to black paper.

ART SPEAK

Your painting technique will vary depending upon the type of snow: light, fluffy snow may be more difficult to work on than frozen, crusted snow. Snow banks with a frozen surface are easiest to paint on, while wet snow makes chalking easier. That's right — all snow is not alike! Try different activities with a variety of snow conditions and materials.

Mix diluted tempera paint, food coloring, or natural food dyes in cans or jugs. Use large brushes or fill old spray bottles with the paints. Experiment using the paints on snow banks. Paint large swirls or bands of color. Rather than painting an object or something you've seen, experiment with color, design, and the shape of the snowbank. What colors look interesting together? How wild can your design get?

Try to work quickly, rather than fussing over the job you are doing. If you don't like it, move on to another snowbank, or pat fresh snow in place over the paint, and try something else.

Colored chalk can be used on snow, too. Break up several pieces of chalk and rub their colors into the wet snow.

4

CREATING TREASURES FROM TRASH

Have you ever looked at garbage with ideas for its potential? Try watching for useful items that would be thrown away around your home — everything from milk containers and yogurt containers to plastic bubble wrap found on many items to microwaveable trays to birthday cards and holiday gift wrap. Use your wonderful imagination and you'll see potential everywhere! How about unraveling the yarn from a sweater that the moths got to or cutting up the fabric from some old curtains? Whatever you save, rinse it out, or fold it up, or wind it around an old tissue tube for safe storage. Keep a "craft box" of reusables in the kitchen or your closet. When you need craft supplies, check out your stashed items.

By being imaginative you can find lots of uses for stuff that would sit for years and years in a landfill. But you also need to think about items before you purchase them. Try to buy only what you need and can use; look for things that aren't packaged in lots of throwaway materials.

Do the earth a favor, and yourself, too, by creating some glorious treasures from trash!

EGG CARTON CUT-UPS

Pulp egg cartons are made from re-cycled paper products and can also be recycled again when you are through using them. Using recycled materials creates jobs, saves natural resources, and lessens the load on our landfills. Best of all, you can have a lot of fun making some wild and crazy cut-ups.

All the egg carton projects are made with the same materials and are at the same degree of difficulty.

✹ ✹ ✹

Materials

Pulp egg cartons
White glue
Paint
Paper clips, toothpicks, straight pins — depending upon project
Scissors

Cut 2 individual egg sections apart; trim the rough edges evenly. These will be the fish's body. Use the carton lid to cut a fin and tail section as shown. Glue the body sections to each side of the fin and tail sections. Hold the pieces together a few minutes until the glue sticks. To make a mouth, cut around one of the pop-up lid fasteners molded into the lower portion of the carton. Glue it on the body.

Paint with tempera. While wet you can sprinkle glitter onto the paint, so it will sparkle like wet fish scales. Decorate the details with markers when the paint is dry. Hang several fish from lengths of old fishing line or string to create a mobile.

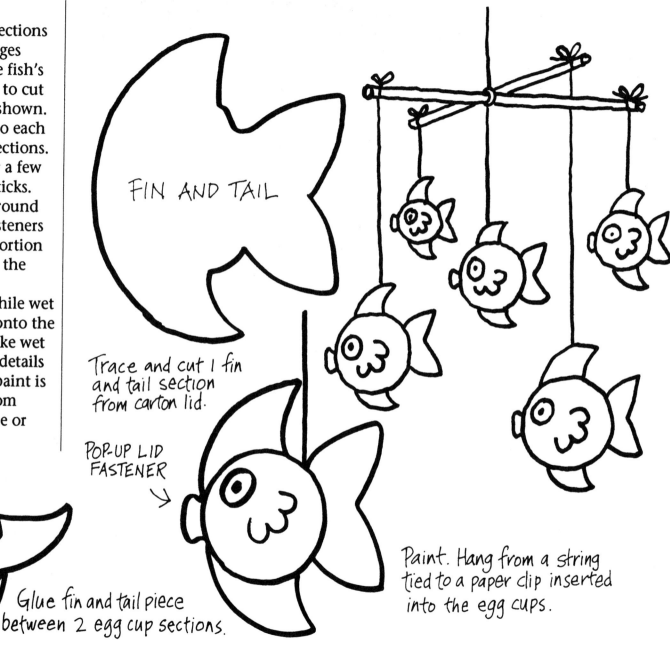

FIN AND TAIL

Trace and cut 1 fin and tail section from carton lid.

POP-UP LID FASTENER

Glue fin and tail piece between 2 egg cup sections.

Paint. Hang from a string tied to a paper clip inserted into the egg cups.

Cut 2 individual egg cup sections apart, leaving little tabs to become feet on one, and leaving 2 tabs for ears on the other. Glue the head section on top of the body section. Break twigs or dry grass and glue on for whiskers.

To create a cat nose, glue a small black pompon, triangle of felt, or cut out the pop-up lid fastener from the carton and glue it in place on top of the whiskers. Paint the cat unusual colors, and glue on a bit of yarn or string for a tail. Can you find some scraps to create a tiny mouse, too?

At the rate Americans are producing garbage, we need 500 new garbage dumps a year.

Cut tabs at 4 corners for feet.

Cut out sides on dotted lines to make 4 legs.

Cut out tabs on another cup for ears.

Glue the head to the body.

Cut 2 individual egg cup sections apart, and trim the rough edges away. Punch 2 holes in the top of one with a nail or sharp pencil. Thread a string through them for suspending the finished plane.

Cut wing and tail sections, and a propeller from the flat carton lid, as shown. Slide the 2 tail sections together at the slit. Now, cut a slit down the side of 1 egg cup section and insert the tail into the slit in the egg cup. Glue the wing section between the 2 cups.

Push a straight pin through the propeller and stick it onto the airplane. Paint as desired with tempera or poster paints. Hang several airplanes from different lengths of string to make a mobile.

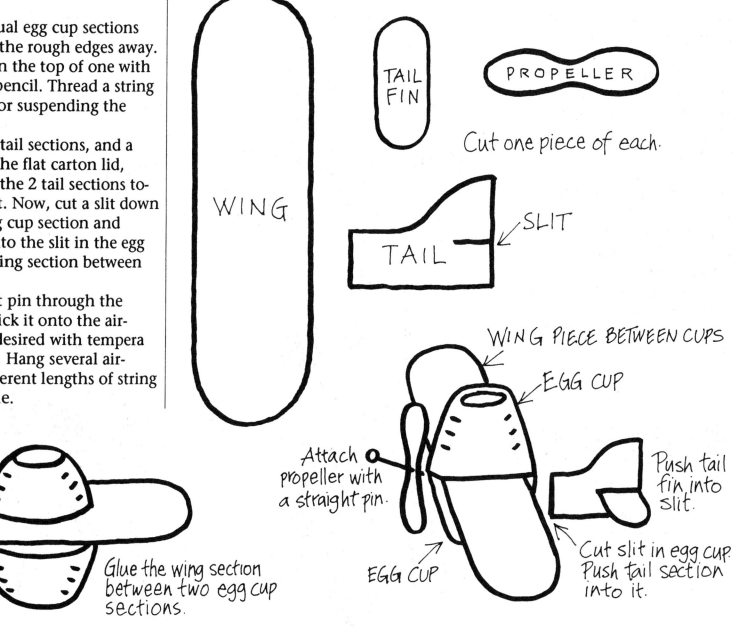

WING

TAIL FIN

PROPELLER

Cut one piece of each.

TAIL — SLIT

WING PIECE BETWEEN CUPS

EGG CUP

Attach propeller with a straight pin.

Push tail fin into slit.

Cut slit in egg cup. Push tail section into it.

EGG CUP

Glue the wing section between two egg cup sections.

SANTA AND SLEIGH

Cut 4 individual egg cups; paint 3 red. Stack and glue them together to create a Santa as shown. Glue on bits of cotton to make the cap, beard, and jacket trim. Paint eyes and buttons, or glue paper cutouts in place.

To make a tiny sleigh, trim another egg cup into a sleigh shape. Paint it red, adding a bit of glitter along the edges for trim. Cut and shape 2 pipe cleaners (or cut out from lid) to make the runners. Glue them in place. Place tiny pine cones or special treats inside the sleigh, and use as a party favor or decoration.

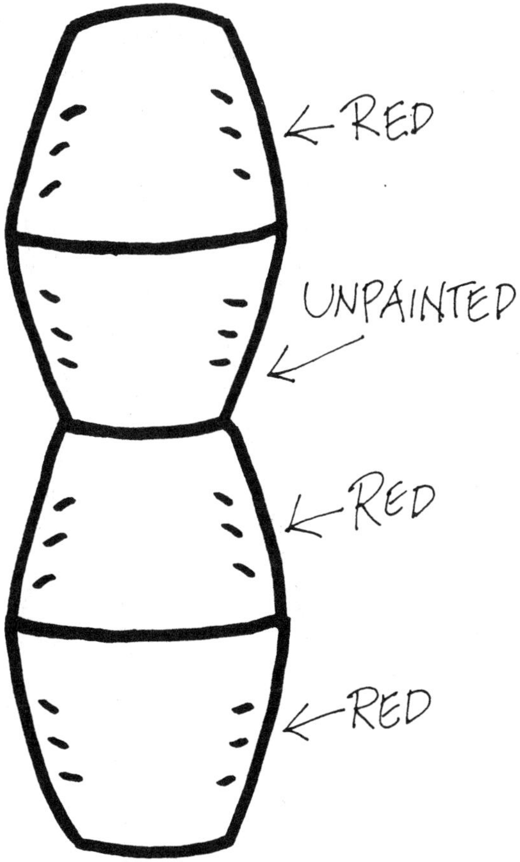

← RED

UNPAINTED

← RED

← RED

Glue cotton balls or stuffing as shown. Decorate with paint or cutouts.

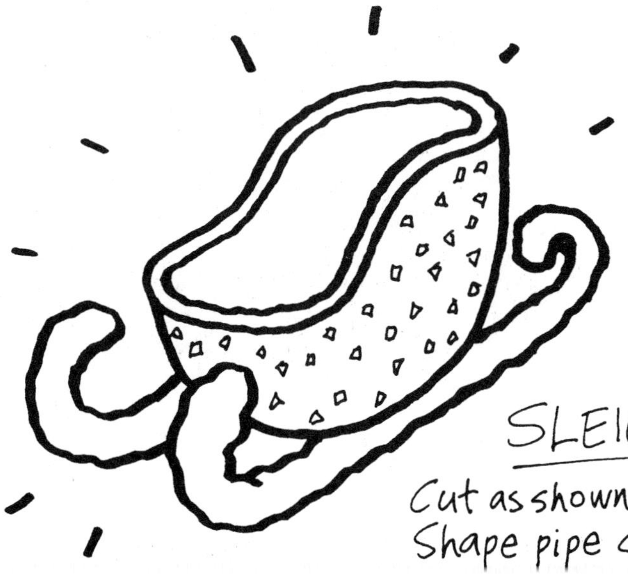

SLEIGH
Cut as shown. Paint and glue on glitter.
Shape pipe cleaner runners and glue in place.

Use the egg cartons with high dividers between cups (rather than rounded ones). Cut a divider section away for the body, leaving turned-up edges for feet.

Cut 2 egg sections and trim away the uneven edges. Glue a cut-out beak between the two head sections. Glue head together, and then the head to the neck of the body. Paint or color with markers, if you wish; then glue on feathers. If you don't have real feathers, make some from cut tissue paper or curl lengths of paper around a pencil and glue in place.

You can make all sorts of egg carton creatures by "building" the basic shape and then adding the trims and details. Try a turtle, or dinosaur, or puppy. Use bits of paper, felt, yarn, and pipe cleaners to give each creative individual details. For eyes, use tiny buttons, beads, seeds, straight pins with black heads, or draw them on with a black pen. Use bits of shag carpet, stuffing, grass, yarn, or string for fur.

Glue together. Paint and glue on paper bag "feathers."

GENEROUS GIFTS & CLEVER CRAFTS

When you reuse discards to make something for someone else, you give two gifts. One is the item you give to the special person, the other gift is to the Earth and all its peoples, by reusing and recycling something that would have become trash.

Not only can you save money by making gifts, you save raw materials that would have gone into making, shipping, and packaging the purchased item. Besides, you get the fun of using your imagination and creativity, while making something you can be proud of. And there is no gift more special to receive than the one made especially by you!

COASTERS

Materials ✳

Yarn

Plastic snap-on lids saved from cans (like coffee and shortening)

Glue

Scissors

Spread glue generously over the inside of the lid. Lay yarn in the glue, working around and around from the outside to the middle. Change colors of yarn, if desired. When the entire lid is yarn-filled, and you are at the center, trim the yarn and tuck the end under to hide it. Let dry.

Great gift for Mom's desk!

DESK ORGANIZER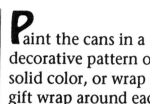

Materials ✳✳

Soup or juice cans, both ends cut out

Glue: latex epoxy

Spray paint, if desired

Clothespins

Paint the cans in a decorative pattern or solid color, or wrap old gift wrap around each can and glue. When dry, glue the cans together to create a pyramid. Use the clothespins to hold the cans securely in place while the glue dries.

Decorate another can to use as a matching pencil holder.

SPECTACULAR FLOWER VASES

Materials ✹✹

Glass bottles or jars with an interesting vase shape

Other materials by choice

Wash out the bottles and let dry. You can then decorate in several ways.

Decoupage: Colorful pictures cut from magazines, scraps from wallpaper, gift wrap, or fabric scraps can be decoupaged by gluing the pictures to the bottle and brushing several coats of white glue over it. Choose a white glue that dries clear and is waterproof. If your glue is too thick to brush on, dilute it with a bit of water.

Waxed: With grown-up help, a lighted candle can be held at an angle, and dripped down the sides of the bottle to make a stunning vase. Try using a variety of colors.

Yarn and grasses: Dip yarn in glue and wrap around the bottle, continuing from the base to the top until the whole bottle is covered. You'll love the results! Grasses can also be dipped in glue and wrapped around the vase, or around a can, for a wonderfully natural look. Dry grass is difficult to use, so gather tall fresh grass. It will shrink tightly around the vase after drying.

Materials

Pulp egg carton

Wire, 6" to 8" long, and button for each flower

Small can or plastic bottle cap (from laundry detergent bottle)

Clay, soil, or plaster of Paris

Gravel, small pebbles, or fluffy moss

Green tissue paper, floral tape, or green construction paper

Scrap of green paper or fabric

Glue and scissors

Cut apart the egg carton, trimming one egg cup into a flower shape. Cut the petals rounded or pointed, depending upon the type of flower you want. Poke 2 small holes in the flower base.

Push the wire up through one hole, through the button, and down through the second hole, threading the button to become the flower's center. Carefully twist the wire ends together, straightening them to make a nice sturdy stem. Cut out paper or fabric leaves, and tape to the wire. Wrap a strip of green tissue paper or

Cut one egg cup into a flower shape.

floral tape around the wire, gluing the ends in place.

Set some clay or soil in the can or lid to anchor the stem, or mix a small amount of plaster of Paris and pour into the can or plastic lid. Position the flower stem as the plaster sets up. Sprinkle gravel or press moss into the surface of the clay or plaster before it hardens, to make it look more decorative. You can also make a bunch of these flowers to put in one of the vases you've made (see page 115) or to "plant" in the patchwork flower pot on the next page.

Thread a button to the center on a wire.

Cut a leaf from green paper. Glue to stem.

Wrap the wire with green paper. Position in a can or plastic cup with clay, soil, or plaster.

PATCH FLOWER POT

Materials ✸

Flower pot: terracotta or reuse a plastic one

White glue and bowl

Fabric scraps: cotton prints with pretty colors and designs

Scissors

Paint brush

Using fabric, you can decoupage an old pot and turn it into something very special with just old fabric scraps and glue.

Cut the fabric into 2" squares. Pour some glue into the bowl and then brush glue on an area of the pot. (If the glue is too thick, add a bit of water to thin it.) Press a fabric piece into the glue. Continue covering the pot with fabric patches, overlapping them so the entire surface of the pot is covered. Now, brush the entire surface with another coat of glue. Let dry. Give the entire pot one more coat of glue to make it nice and shiny.

Now it's ready to fill with rich soil and cuttings or seeds, or some of your egg carton flowers (see page 116)!

NAPKIN RINGS ➤➤ ➤➤

Materials ✸

Paper tubes

Cloth or gift wrap scraps

Glue

Scissors or pinking shears, if desired

Ask a grown-up to help cut the paper tubes into sections about an inch wide.

If you are using pinking shears, cut the fabric and paper into small pieces, about 1" x 1". Glue on the pieces and press them in place to cover the tubes, inside and out. Glue on bits of yarn, lace, braid, or feathers for decoration. Nuts and evergreen sprigs make nice autumn touches.

Cut rings.

Cover with scraps.

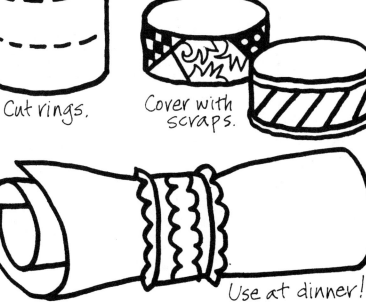

Use at dinner!

MAGAZINE HOLDER

Materials ✹✹✹

Large cereal box or detergent box

Something to cover the box with: gift wrap, adhesive paper, leftover latex paint, or fabric

Glue, if needed

Ruler

Cut the box at an angle, as shown in the illustration, leaving about 4" at the shorter side. Use the ruler to be sure both sides are even. Paint, or cut fabric or paper and glue on to cover.

Cut box sides. Decorate.

NIFTY NOTE PAD ➡

Materials ✹

Papers

Yarn or ribbon

Hole punch or stapler

paper, gift wrap, or colored construction paper) over a stack of smaller papers to form a header.

Punch holes and tie with yarn or ribbon. Or, staple it and glue on a ribbon to cover the staples.

Decorate the top sheet with crayon designs, prints (see page 85), or rubber stamps. Use as an assignment pad, address book, or for telephone messages.

This is an easy way to use up small-size papers. Fold a larger piece of colored paper (wall-

LITTLE WORLDS

Our planet Earth is really very small when compared to the rest of the universe. It's our home, and we need to be as careful with it as we can. We're all living in one community, and how each one of us lives affects all of the other living things. The amount of fresh water and the number of growing trees are really very small when compared to living things depending on these resources. We need to use what we have left wisely.

One way to do this is to look at objects around your house with imagination and a creative eye. Boxes, tubes, cans, containers can all be used to make something out of nothing. All it takes is the simple step of looking at a common object and asking yourself, "How many different ways can I use this?"

Materials

Reused cardboard boxes

Tissue tubes in assorted sizes

Tempera paint, or leftover latex house paint

Scissors

White glue

Cut a large cardboard base to glue your castle to from a large carton. You may want to look in a few books for some details from real castles, or simply use your imagination.

Assemble the boxes and cans, arranging and re-arranging, until you have an idea of how your castle might look. Once everything is arranged to your liking, begin the construction by gluing the bottom boxes to the base. Use white glue, or, with a grown-up's help, use a hot glue gun.

Use boxes, tubes, and cans to create a castle.

SHOE BOX CASTLE

You can make towers by using scissors to cut paper tubes, or use frozen juice cans. A paper half-circle can be taped into a cone to roof the towers. Cardboard can be cut for a drawbridge that pulls up and down on lengths of yarn. You can create colorful flags from fabric scraps glued to twigs and stuck in the roof. And this is just the beginning . . . the possibilities are endless.

Once all the glue is dry, paint the finished castle with leftover latex paint or tempera.

To make a shoe box castle, use shoe boxes and tissue tubes. Cover the outside of the box and the tissue tubes with paint or colored paper. Glue a tube in each corner of the box. Cut colored paper in half circles and glue on top of the tubes for tower roofs. Cut paper triangles and tape to twigs for flags.

Materials ❦❦

Boxes, large ones for the house, small for furniture

Glue

Fabric and wallpaper scraps, used gift-wrap

Small caps, spools, lids

Leftover latex paint, brush

Hot glue gun (for grown-up use) or heavy adhesive

Glue boxes together. Fold a cardboard roof and glue on.

Dolls of any size can be comfortable in houses created from cardboard cartons. Create a house with different floor levels to suit your needs, by gluing two or three boxes together. A hot glue gun used by a grown-up works best, but heavy-duty adhesive will work, too.

Give the cartons a coat or two of leftover latex paint. It helps make the house look great and strengthens the cardboard. A roof can be made by scoring a large flat piece of cardboard down the center, and then folding to create a roof. Ask a grown-up to glue the top onto the house with a hot glue gun.

Begin searching and scrounging for decorating materials to give the house its personality. Select heavy fabric scraps like felt and toweling for carpeting. Used gift wrap or pieces of extra wall paper (sometimes you can get an old sample book from a store) can be glued in place to cover the walls.

You can cut out rectangles and glue on windows made from pieces of clear acetate saved from packaging materials. Cut out tiny pictures from magazines to hang as paintings on the walls. Make mirrors by gluing pieces of old aluminum foil to cardboard.

Make the furniture from small boxes and spools. Glue them together to create dressers, tables, chairs, and sofas. Use lids from jars, plastic tubs, and screw-on caps as platters, bowls, lamps, basins, or flower pots.

Fabric scraps become tablecloths, bedding, and curtains. A twig stuck in a bottle cap filled with modeling clay becomes a houseplant. Food can be shaped from homemade play dough.

The more materials you gather, the more ideas you will generate for additional furniture and decorations. The secret is to build and furnish your house with materials that would end up in the trash.

CAP LAMPSHADE

SPOOL AND LID TABLE

Glue beads on a box for a dresser.

Cut out small magazine pictures for paintings.

Glue moss in a cap for a houseplant.

Materials

Several small boxes, different sizes and shapes

Colored paper

Paint and brushes; marking pens

Assorted items you have saved to reuse

Tape, glue, and scissors

Save small boxes, such as different-sized milk cartons, until you have enough to create several buildings. Think about shapes for houses, stores, post office, a school, fire station, church, synagogue, or whatever else you would like in your town. Your town can look like a typical town, or you may want to develop a town from the Wild West, or imagine a town on Mars!

You may want some construction paper, paints, marking pens, straws, tissue tubes, buttons, twigs, clay, and assorted reusable odds and ends for the details.

The boxes can be painted with tempera or leftover latex paint. Add

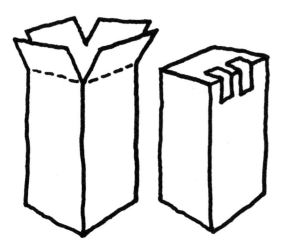

Cut slits in carton top. Fold down and tape.

Cut 1 milk carton to make the roof. Cut out the side of another milk carton for the base. Tape. Cut and fold doors and windows.

CARTON COTTAGE

Tape top closed. Glue on a folded rectangle of colored paper for a roof. Glue on colored paper siding, windows, and doors.

a little liquid detergent to help the paint adhere to the boxes better. Or, you can tape or glue paper to cover the boxes, or just leave the boxes as they are.

It's fun to arrange the houses on a table top or floor, or outdoors in a sandpile. If you want to create a mat to set your town on, use an old plastic shower curtain or a sheet. Draw the streets and parks with a permanent marking pen. The mat can be rolled up when you are not playing with it.

To create a simple house from a milk carton, tape it at the top. Glue on a folded rectangle of construction paper for the roof. Cut a door and windows, or just paint them on.

A larger house can be made from two milk cartons. Cut one to make the roof, and the side of another for the base. Tape them together. Cut and fold doors and windows.

Larger boxes can become apartment buildings. Draw many windows with a heavy marking pen, or paste on several small paper rectangles.

Use short pieces of shrubbery for trees. Stick the ends in balls of modeling clay. Street lights can be made by squeezing used scraps of aluminum foil to one end of a drinking straw and pressing the other end into modeling clay. You can even make a cobblestone sidewalk by gluing pebbles or shells to cardboard.

Make people by drawing faces on Popsicle sticks, gluing on clothing cut from fabric scraps or paper, and pushing the sticks into balls of modeling clay for support.

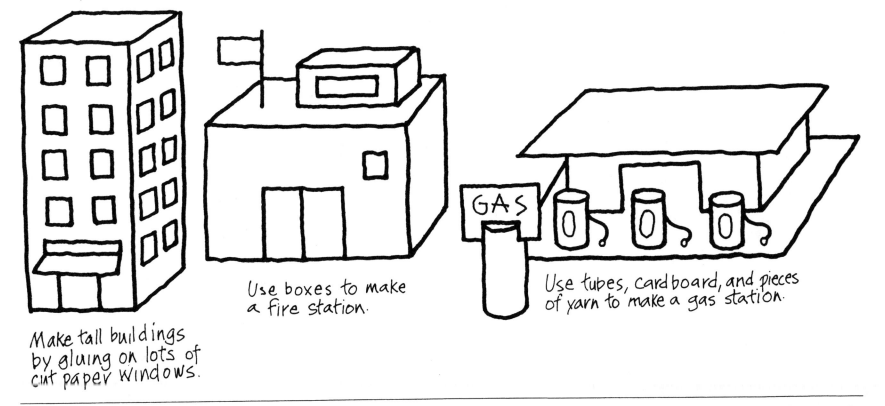

Make tall buildings by gluing on lots of cut paper windows.

Use boxes to make a fire station.

GAS

Use tubes, cardboard, and pieces of yarn to make a gas station.

Materials ✹✹

Large cardboard carton, from furniture or appliances

Serrated knife, for grown-up use

Leftover latex paint, optional

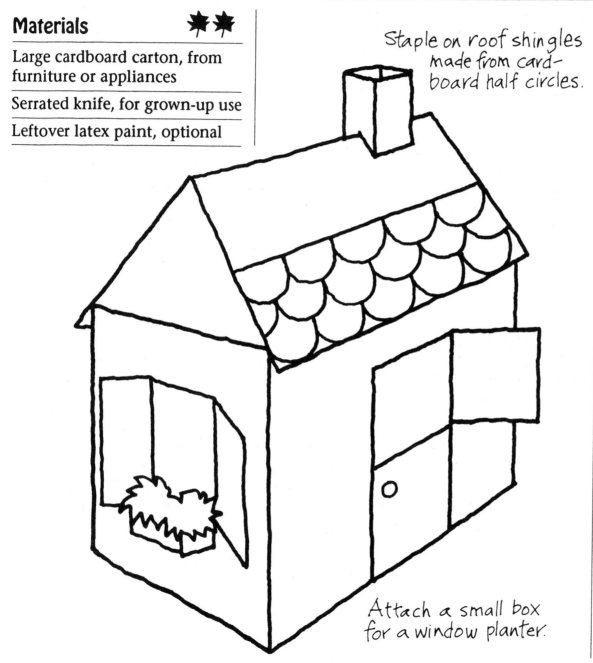

Staple on roof shingles made from cardboard half circles.

Attach a small box for a window planter.

Large-sized play houses that you and your friends can play in can be made from large, corrugated cartons, obtained from appliance stores. Ask a grown-up to help you cut out any door or window areas you want with a serrated knife.

The house can be painted with leftover latex paint, or left as is. Cut a large piece of cardboard, fold in half, and attach for a roof. Trace large circles (about the size of a dinner plate) onto thin cardboard or copier paper you have saved. Cut out, cut them in half, and staple in overlapping rows to create roof shingles.

A window box can be attached beneath the window; just staple or glue a shoe box in place and fill it with greenery — real or your creation. Narrow boxes can be stacked on top of each other, end to end, and glued in place for a chimney.

Your play house can be anything you think of — a fort, cabin, castle, igloo, or space shuttle. Decorate with whatever you have on hand. When you are through with the house, take it to a cardboard bundler for recycling.

PLASTIC JUG CRAFTS

Plastic jugs are everywhere, it seems. Look around your home, and you will find them holding water, milk, soda pop, syrup, juice, and more. If you rinse them out and squash them flat (use your foot to stomp them), you can save them for the recycling center. Some plastics are now being recycled into heavier plastic items, such as fencing materials, park benches, even home insulation. If your recycling center doesn't take plastic, ask your parents to find one that does.

Before you send all the jugs to the recycling center, here are a few ways you can create (instead of buying) some fun and useful things — in the true spirit of environmental awareness.

Plastic bottles can be cut with scissors or a craft knife (you may want to ask for grown-up help). Sand the rough edges with sandpaper, if needed. Decorate with markers, glued on fabrics, or paints.

Note: Projects vary from one to three leaves in skill levels, once the jugs have been cut by a grown-up.

SCOOPS

Cut different-sized bottles to make useful scoops for the sandbox or beach.

Cut a milk jug to make a scoop.

Tape a "ball" from old newspapers to make a toss and catch game.

FUNNEL

Cut a bottle in half, and use the top half for a funnel in the sand box, wading pool, or bathtub.

Cut from any size bottle.

Use to fill containers.

FLOWER POT

The bottom half of a jug or large bottle makes a good flower pot. Decorate it with marking pens, stickers, or leftover paint. Cut a scallop edge along the top, and use a hole punch to create a decorative design. Use a hole punch to place four holes equal distances around the top edge. Tie on yarn or heavy cord to make a hanging planter.

Punch 2 holes; tie on a cord. Decorate and fill with hanging plants.

Cut the edge in scallops. Punch holes for decoration.

DOOR STOP

Fill a bottle with sand, fasten the lid on with strong glue, and color with markers to make a door stop.

DOLL HOUSE OR GAS STATION

Make a portable doll house or a gas station for small toy cars. Cut a large window in the side of the bottle, leaving about 1/2" along the top and bottom of the bottle and going about half-way across the bottle. Decorate the outside with permanent markers. Glue scraps of cloth or colored papers inside. For dolls, make furniture from small boxes and spools. Make a fuel pump for the cars by punching a hole with a nail and tying on a length of shoelace for a fuel hose.

Cut.

Cut, fold down.

Bend wire for TV antenna.

Decorate with markers.

Use fabric scraps for carpet, spools, and boxes for furniture.

PIGGY BANK

Of course, the piggy bank is traditional. Collect four wine corks and a half-gallon bottle. You'll need fabric or leather scraps for ears, and a pipe cleaner or fabric scrap for the tail.

To make the legs, cut four circles the size of the wine corks in the side of the bottle. Push the corks in firmly, adding glue if necessary. Cut a slit in the top of the pig for the coins. Cut a slash for inserting the triangle-shaped ears into the pig; add glue if needed. Punch a hole in the rear with a nail and insert the tail. Give it a curl. Paint the entire pig pink or cover with papier-mache made from newspaper strips dipped in flour and water glue. Finish by gluing or painting on eyes.

What else could your bank become? How about an armadillo bank or a porcupine bank? Decorate with paint or pieces of colored papers.

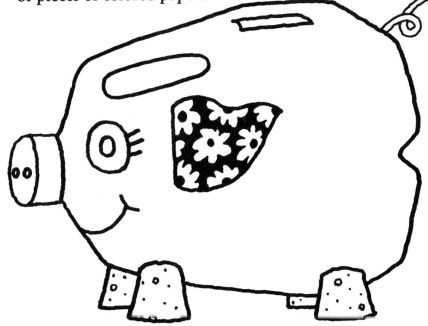

WATERING CAN

Make a watering can for the garden by punching holes near the top of the bottle with a sharp nail. Decorate with markers or stickers.

Punch holes with large nails. Fill with water and give your garden a drink!

BASKET

You can make a lovely basket by cutting away the lower part of a jug, and then cutting vertical slits in the side. Make an even number of slits. Cut them about 3/4" apart. Use fabric strips to weave in and out between the slits, continuing around the bottle until the slits are filled in. Use the top of the bottle to cut a handle. Punch holes in the handle ends and the sides of the basket and use brass paper fasteners or pieces of yarn to tie the handle in place. Omit the slits and weaving, and you'll have a beach bucket.

Cut slits and weave fibers through.

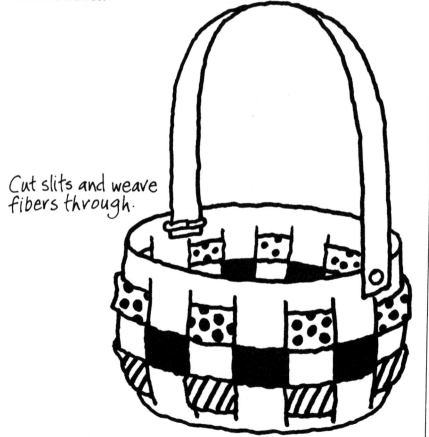

MASKS

Large milk bottles are perfect masks. The handle can become a nose; cut out large circles for eyes (always make sure you can see in your mask). Decorate with leftover paints, dimensional fabric paints, or permanent marking pens. Glue on cut-out shapes from colored papers, gift wrap, or paper bags. To create hair around the edges of the mask, use a hole punch to punch holes about 3/8" apart along the top edge. Knot loops of yarn through the holes, pulling to secure (see Homemade Yarn, page 27). To keep the mask in place, punch two holes at the sides and tie a piece of elastic braid through the holes, or staple it in place at the sides.

Cut top and bottom edges. Cut out eyes, and mouth.

BOTTLE DOLL

Turn a bottle into a doll, ghost, or fairy tale character. Use a two-liter bottle for a slender figure, a gallon jug for a chubbier one.

Weight the bottle with some sand or gravel, and glue the lid on securely. Make the head by wadding stuffing in the end of a sock and tying securely. Slip this down over the neck of the bottle and tie in place with heavy string. Make the face with paint, embroidery, or by gluing on cut pieces of felt. Dust the cheeks with powder blusher. Hair can be made from wool, stuffing, yarn, or narrow strips of torn fabric. Sew or glue in place. Create clothing from scraps.

Stuff a sock and tie, then glue in place.

GRAVEL INSIDE BOTTLE

Make hair from torn strips of cloth or yarn. Dress in fabric remnants glued in place.

FUN & GAMES

There are lots of reasons why "new" toys aren't always best: their manufacture, packaging, and shipping place an additional burden on the earth; they cost money that we can use for other things; and they eventually break or bore us and find their way into the landfill.

Sometimes homemade toys — made out of reusable and recycled materials — have a special something that the shiniest new toy doesn't have. Making these toys is half of the fun, and playing with them is the other half! Giving them as gifts provides added satisfaction. As if that is not enough, you are doing something good for the earth.

BEAN BAG TOSS

Materials ★ ★ ★

Strong cloth (a good way to use old denim jeans)

Dry beans: soybeans, pinto, or navy beans

Plastic soda bottles (various sizes)

Cardboard box

Sewing machine (optional)

Needle, thread, and scissors

Here's a great game you can make yourself — all with recycled materials. To make each bean bag, cut 2 identical pieces of fabric, with the right sides facing each other. The easiest shape is a 5" square. An adult can sew the pieces together or show you how to do it. Leave a 2" opening for filling with the beans.

Trim the corners away, close to the stitching. Turn the bag right side out through the opening. Put about a cup of beans into each bag; it should be loosely filled and sort of limp. Turn the edges of the fabric in and handstitch the opening closed with small stitches.

Simple, sturdy bean bags are just plain fun to toss around. Create games of skill by cutting different-sized plastic jugs in half and tossing the bags into them. Cut holes in the side of a large cardboard box, and toss bean bags through the holes. Label the holes or jugs with numbers, and tally up everyone's scores.

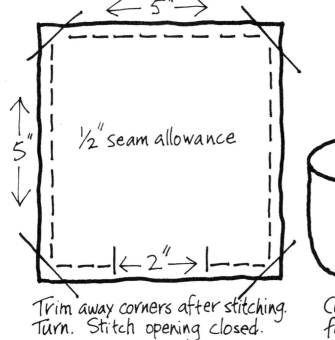

Trim away corners after stitching. Turn. Stitch opening closed.

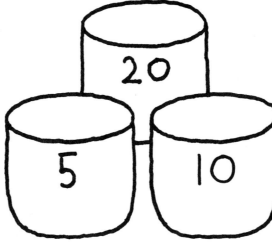

Cut plastic bottles and label for a toss game.

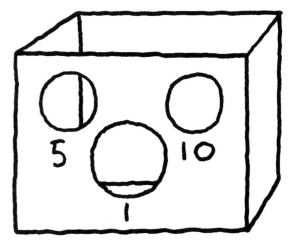

Cut holes in the sides of a box. Label with points.

Materials ✿✿

Large, paper, grocery bag

Tape, string, scissors

Pencil

Hole punch (optional)

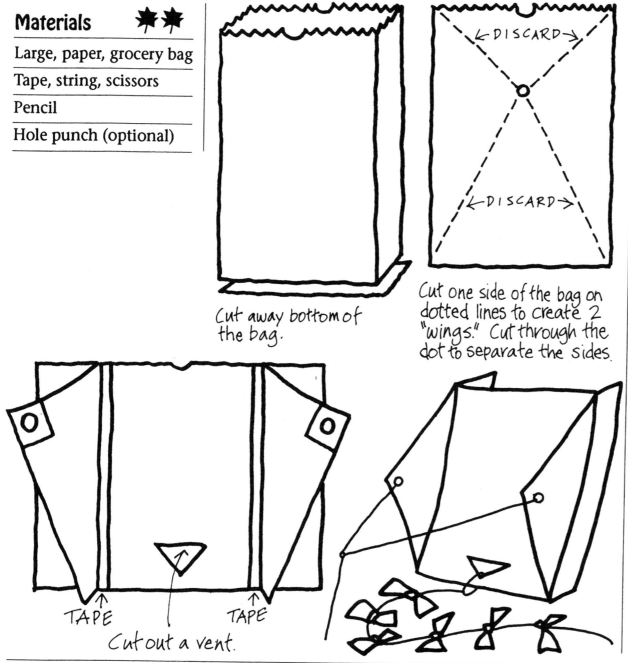

Cut away bottom of the bag.

Cut one side of the bag on dotted lines to create 2 "wings." Cut through the dot to separate the sides.

TAPE   TAPE

Cut out a vent.

The best thing about this kite is that you probably have all of the materials you need in your house right now. You also don't need to obtain any sticks.

Cut the bottom out of the bag. Lay the bag flat on the table top. Pencil a dot about 1/3 down from the top center of the bag. Draw wings from the corners to that dot. Cut away the top and bottom triangle areas, cutting along the dotted lines, as shown.

Turn the bag over, and fold the wings to the front. Tape them to the bag. Put a piece of tape at the tip of each wing to strengthen it; then, punch a hole through it.

Cut out a triangle-shaped vent near the bottom of the bag. A tail made from pieces of tissue tied on a string can be tied below the vent.

Be sure to decorate your kite before flying. Short streamers can be cut from tissue paper and glued or stapled in place.

CAN WALKERS

Materials ✹✹

.2 cans the same size: 48-ounce juice cans are good

6' – 8' of rope, cut in 2 equal lengths

Punch-type can opener

These are simple to make and great fun to use. They're not too difficult to walk on and are perfect for a backyard Olympics or circus.

Remove the tops of the cans. Punch 2 holes in the sides of each can, just below the rim, directly across from each other. Thread the rope through the holes and knot securely.

To use, stand on the end near the holes and hold the ropes in each hand. Try walking. Practice makes perfect!

Punch 2 holes in closed end of cans.

OPEN END

Thread rope through the holes, and knot.

OPEN END

CHECKERS GAME

Materials

24 small, flat, plastic lids: 12 of each color (save the plastic lids from milk, water, and juice bottles)

Large cardboard pizza box, at least 16" x 16" inside

Paint or markers in two colors

Ruler and pencil

Rule the cardboard inside the box into 64 two-inch squares (see illustration). There should be 8 squares down each side. Color or paint alternating squares so you have a checkerboard pattern.

Line up the opposing game pieces on each side of the board (12 lids for each player) and let the game begin! When you are finished, store the game pieces inside the box.

Use a pizza box and milk bottle caps.

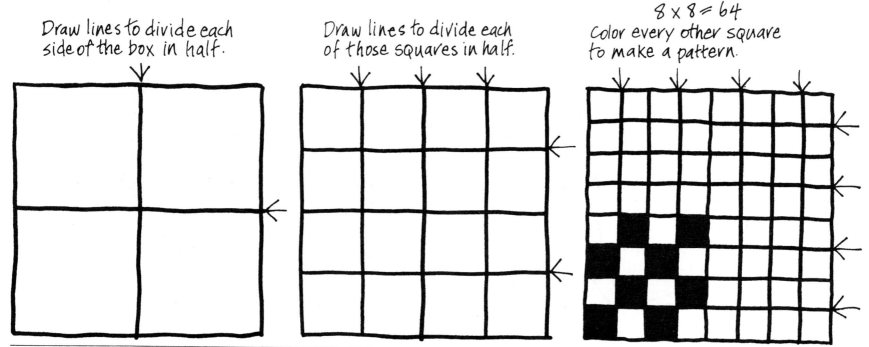

HERE'S HOW TO MAKE 64 SQUARES

Draw lines to divide each side of the box in half.

Draw lines to divide each of those squares in half.

Draw lines to divide each of those squares in half. There will be 8 on each side.
8 x 8 = 64
Color every other square to make a pattern.

BOX PUZZLES

Materials ★★★🦆

9 or more small, identical boxes: raisin, pudding, or gelatin boxes are ideal

Old magazine

Paste (see Pastes & Glues, page 24)

Tape

Pencil and ruler

Scissors

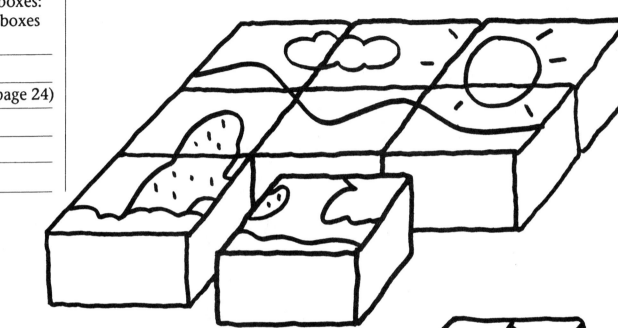

Tape the boxes closed. Lay the boxes out to create a rectangle or square.

Find a picture in a magazine that is colorful and fun, and that is the size of all of the boxes together. If you want, you can draw a picture yourself, using plenty of interesting design and color.

Use the ruler to measure and divide the picture into sections the size of each box. Cut the picture and glue each section to one side of each box. This will be one side of your puzzle.

Keeping the boxes in place, turn each over to the other side, and cut and glue sections from another picture on the other side of the box. Now, mix the boxes up and see if you can put them back in order to solve the puzzle.

To make the pieces last longer, you can cover the finished boxes with a coat of white glue diluted with water, or with clear adhesive paper.

Puppets are such a great, fun-filled way to enjoy art and drama. A puppet can be made from just about anything. Search through your box of odds and ends, your button box, and you're sure to find just what you need to make a one-of-a-kind puppet creation. ✹

Finger puppets

These are the simplest to create. Draw faces on your fingertips or on your hand with fine-tip marking pens. You can also draw on peanut shells or paper strips that are taped and worn on your fingertips.

Stick puppets

Sticks can be Popsicle sticks, paint stirring sticks, or long twigs. You can also roll a newspaper page tightly into a tube and tape. Draw your puppets on paper or cardboard; decorate with markers or paint. Hair can be cut from yarn, moss, fabric, or curled paper strips. Glue or staple in place. Tape or glue the puppet to the stick.

Glue drawings to sticks for puppets.

Decorate your hands for the easiest hand puppets.

Box puppets

These puppets have mouths that move. Use a small box, like a gelatin box. Cut one side down the center and sides. Fold the ends of the boxes back, and you have a mouth. Cover with colored paper or paint. You can glue feathers, cut paper, yarn, or whatever you have for decoration.

Cut a box in half on 3 sides. Decorate, fold, and put your fingers inside to make it move.

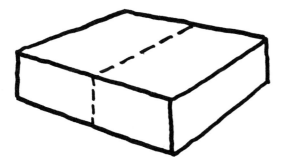

Cut and fold cardboard oval in half.

Glue inside sock. Decorate and slip over your hand.

Sock puppets

Here is a fun way to use old socks. They just naturally lend themselves to becoming arm puppets. To create a working mouth, cut an oval from cardboard, score it down the center, and fold. Insert the cardboard into the sock's toe, and glue it in place for a mouth. Sew on buttons for eyes, or cut shapes from felt and glue in place. Use your imagination and create all sorts of wild and crazy characters. Then put on a great puppet show.

Envelope puppets

Old envelopes make instant puppets, too. Tape an envelope closed. Fold it in half, and cut one side open along the fold. Insert your fingers in one section and your thumb in the other. Decorate with crayons, markers, or pieces of colored paper.

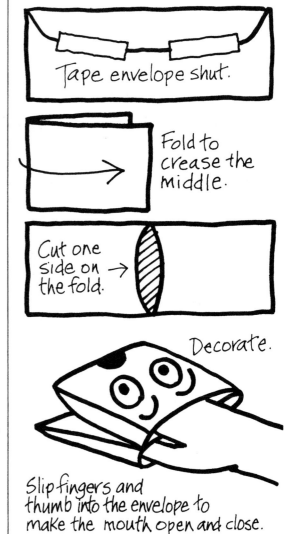

Tape envelope shut.

Fold to crease the middle.

Cut one side on the fold. →

Decorate.

Slip fingers and thumb into the envelope to make the mouth open and close.

Puppet Stage

If you have a large cardboard carton, you can cut out a window, hang a cloth for a curtain, and give a real show. You can also stretch a sheet across a table or chair, or stretch a clothesline between trees and hang a tablecloth.

Cut a box for a stage.

MY THEATER

SHOW TIMES 1:00 AND 2:00

NOW SHOWING LITTLE RED RIDINGHOOD

BOOMERANG

Australians invented the boomerang, which is a flat, curved shape that can be thrown so that it returns to the thrower.

Materials ✹✹

Cardboard

Scissors

Pencil

Draw and cut a boomerang shape from the cardboard. Decorate with markers or paint. You may want to change the design a bit, making several in different sizes and shapes. Toss and compare how they soar.

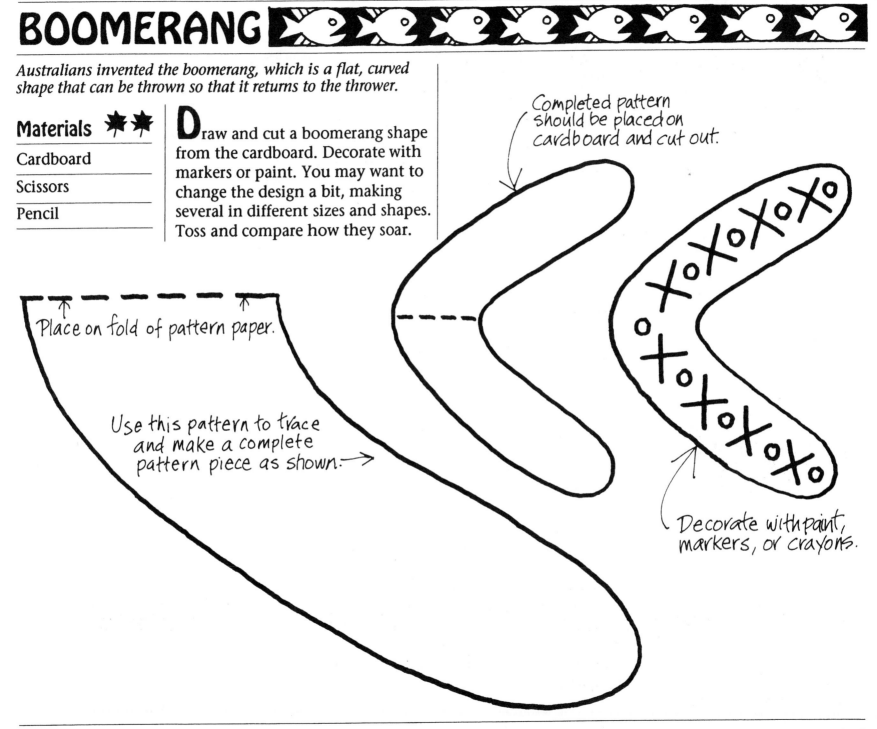

Place on fold of pattern paper.

Use this pattern to trace and make a complete pattern piece as shown. →

Completed pattern should be placed on cardboard and cut out.

Decorate with paint, markers, or crayons.

GIFTS FOR THE EARTH

Although every project in this book has helped the earth by reusing and recycling, here are some creations that are fun to make, but that also save our natural resources.

The following projects will begin to change your family's habits. Once you make your family a set of cloth napkins, you won't need to purchase disposable paper ones, made from our majestic forests. Saving recyclables in your own bin saves natural resources, prevents overfilling the land-fills, and creates jobs in the recycling industry. By creating compost, you are recycling nutrients and developing good "earth" that will nourish plants and living things.

These projects are certainly fun to make with your family, but using them together is where the real satisfaction comes. By choosing these alternate lifestyle activities, you are doing something positive and lasting. It won't be the efforts of business or industry that change our quality of life. It will be our individual efforts, small but consistent, that change the tide. Little things do mean a lot.

INSPIRATION BOX

Materials

Assorted boxes including 2 large ones

Paints and permanent markers

Make a box just for those unusual things you find now and then that might be useful in art and craft projects. Find a sturdy carton and decorate it to suit your personality: perhaps graffiti with markers, or a collage cut from magazines. Add a few smaller boxes to keep tiny findings inside — like small shells you have gathered, unusual pebbles, or buttons you've collected. Ask your family to help you watch for useful items. A broken necklace, pretty stamps or stickers from the mail, corks, magnets, fake flowers, fabric remnants, yarn, gift wrap, and ribbons — whatever you come across that might be useful some day — can be saved until you are ready for it.

You'll also want to keep a separate, larger box to store clean jars, margarine tubs, and yogurt containers, tissue rolls, egg cartons, styrofoam meat trays (rinse in hot water first), and pieces of foil you have sponged off and folded flat. Paint or decorate it and write "Crafts" on it.

CLOTH NAPKINS

Materials

Fabric: woven cotton is best

Scissors

Sewing machine, or needle and thread

What a great way to add sophistication to your meals, while saving trees that would be cut down for paper pulp! As a logger once said, "We are the only people that grind up our forests to wipe our mouths."

Years ago, everyone had cloth napkins. In the Pilgrim's time they used large napkins that were draped over their shoulders while eating.

You can make a whole set of cloth napkins for your family. Buy some woven cotton broadcloth fabric remnants at a fabric store (each napkin can be from different fabric), or better yet, recycle an old sheet, curtain, or dress.

To make napkins, cut the fabric into 17" x 17" squares, one for each napkin. If you have a sewing machine, ask a grown-up to help you turn the edges under and stitch

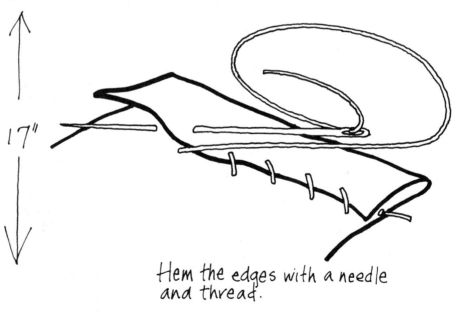

Cut a 17" square.

Hem the edges with a needle and thread.

them down, making a hem. If not, you can roll the cut fabric edges under, and stitch them in place with a needle and thread. (If you don't know how to sew yet, this is an easy project for you to learn the basic hemming stitch.)

When your squares are all hemmed, you can use old pieces of sponge, or cut shapes from potatoes to print designs on the napkins with acrylic or fabric paints, or your own home-made natural dyes (see page16).

Put the napkins into napkin rings you have made for everyone in your family (see page 117), or put names on the napkins. Then, there will be a personal napkin for everyone, and you won't have to wash the napkins after every meal.

After you have completed making the napkins, fold them up neatly and place them in an old basket, or decorate the outside of an empty coffee can or shoe box. Your family can store them there — each with its own napkin ring — keeping them ready for the next meal.

Paint or print designs on the napkins.

DYES

RECYCLING BINS

Set a good example for your family by creating recycling bins and then using them! If you do this, chances are your whole family will join in the effort, and you will have moved everyone in your family one step closer to being good earth citizens.

Try to place your bins where they are accessible, but not in the way. Talk over the place to keep them with your parents. Offer to go on the weekly visit to the nearest recycling center, too. Your interest in making recycling work in your home will be a real gift to the earth.

Materials ✦✦

Large cardboard boxes

Leftover latex paint, or used gift wrap

Permanent markers

Cord and scissors

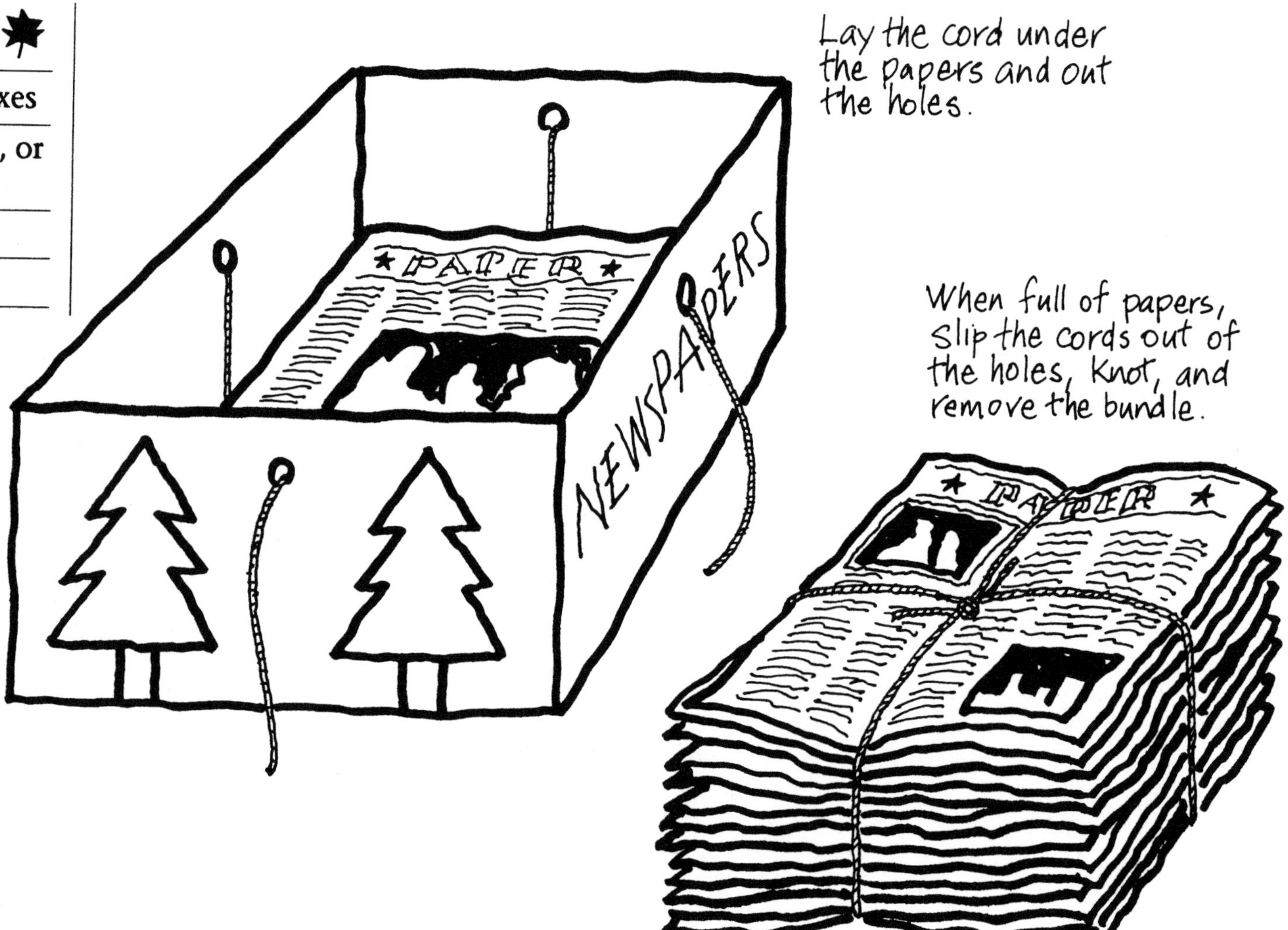

Lay the cord under the papers and out the holes.

When full of papers, slip the cords out of the holes, knot, and remove the bundle.

Create separate storage areas for the variety of items you recycle. Save sturdy cardboard boxes and paint them with leftover latex house paint, which gives the cardboard more strength and makes them look special, too. Or, decorate them with used gift wrap. Make separate boxes for aluminum, for plastics, and for glass, clearly labelling each one with a permanent marker. Make a small box to put near the computer or typewriter for saving white bond paper.

Now, make a special box for newspapers by punching holes in the four sides near the top of the box, and then placing the cord across the inside of the box and up through the holes. Pile in the newspapers each day, until it's full, and then just pull the loose ends of cord from the holes and tie securely to bundle. Slide the bundle out of the box to take to the recycling center, and restring the box for the next pile of newspapers.

COMPOST HOLDER

Materials

Large plastic jug from milk or water

Permanent markers or paints

Scissors or serrated knife

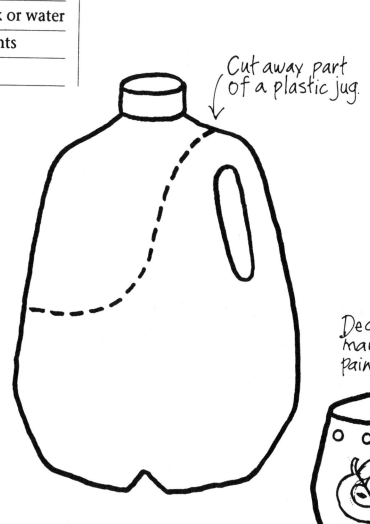

Cut away part of a plastic jug.

Make a compost holder by cutting a large opening in a plastic bottle, as shown. Draw on fruits and veggies with permanent markers. Keep the holder by the sink for food scraps (no bones or meat), and carry it out to dump on your compost heap in the yard after dinner. Your holder can be washed with hot, soapy water and reused each day.

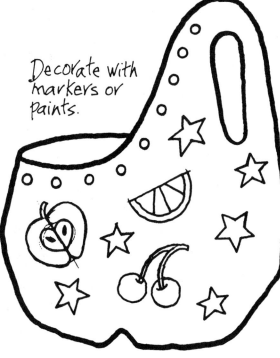

Decorate with markers or paints.

DRAFT DODGER

Make a crazy-looking snake that will help you stay warm and save energy, too. Place it across the bottom of doors and windows to prevent warm air from escaping in winter, or cool air escaping in the summer.

Materials ✹✹

Old tights

Rags or old clothing

Needle and thread

Scraps of felt and glue

Cut a leg off the old tights. Stuff with cut-up pieces of old clothing or rags. Stitch the end closed. Glue on some felt pieces for eyes and mouth. Decorate with pieces of felt to make an attractive, playful critter.

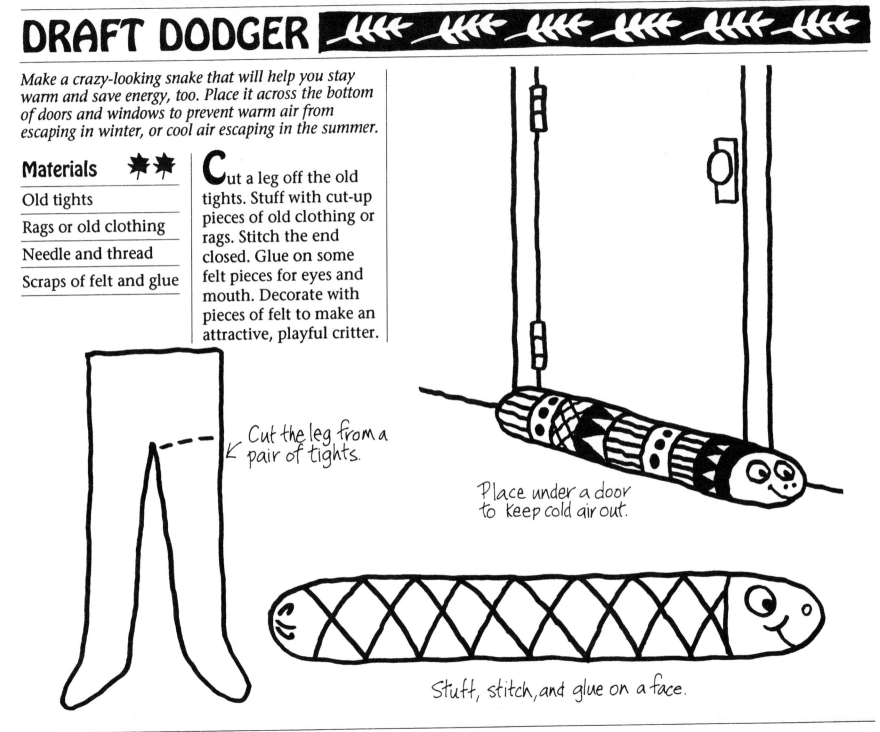

Cut the leg from a pair of tights.

Place under a door to keep cold air out.

Stuff, stitch, and glue on a face.

SHOPPING BAG

Cloth shopping bags are useful as well as ecologically sound. You won't have to decide between "paper or plastic," and your bag can be folded up and carried in a purse or pocket. Make up several for gifts or to sell in a money-making venture for your club or group.

Materials

Heavy canvas or denim fabric

Sewing machine or needle and thread

Scissors

You can do this "by hand," but it really is easier with a sewing machine. Ask a grown-up to help you. Cut the fabric to the following dimensions: 38" x 18" rectangle for the bag, and two 4" x 12" pieces for handles.

Fold the rectangle in half, right side of fabric facing inside, and stitch the side together. Now, re-fold the bag so the seam is in the center, and stitch the bottom. Use a double row of stitching to make it sturdy.

1. Fold and stitch side seam of the bag.

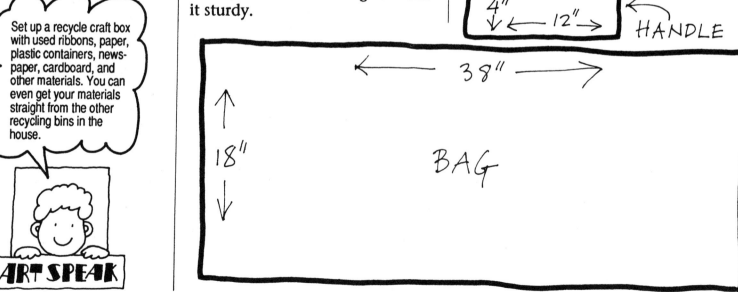

4" ← 12" → HANDLE

← 38" →

18"

BAG

Set up a recycle craft box with used ribbons, paper, plastic containers, newspaper, cardboard, and other materials. You can even get your materials straight from the other recycling bins in the house.

ART SPEAK

Pull the bag up at the ends to create two triangular corner areas. Stitch across these ends with a double seam.

Turn the bag right side out and hem the top edge.

Make the handles by sewing a seam down the center of each smaller rectangle. Turn right side out and stitch securely to each side of the bag.

Decorate the finished bag with fabric or acrylic paints. Use a cut-up sponge or potato to print with acrylic paints. Tie dye or paint with your homemade dyes (see page 16).

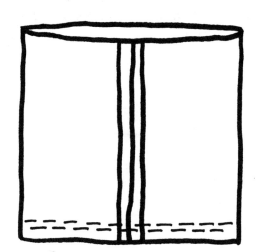

Fold and stitch bottom of bag.

Simple shopping bags can be made from the mesh bags that onions and potatoes are sold in. Remove the paper labels and decorate by weaving or stitching with colorful yarn and a yarn needle. Run a piece of heavy cord or leather boot lace through the top to make a drawstring.

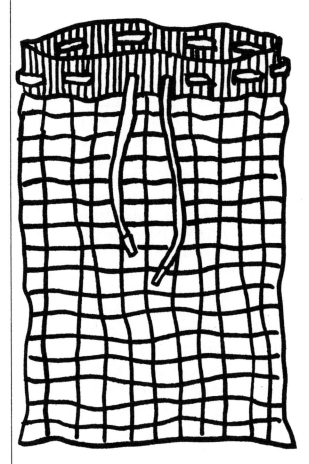

Fold corners out and stitch across them.

Turn. Hem top. Sew on handles. Decorate with markers or paint.

RAG BAG

Materials ★★

Old pillowcase

Piece of rope

Needle and thread

Permanent markers or homemade dyes (see page 16)

Work the rope through the casing.

Tie the ends and hang.

Make a rag bag for your family by using an old pillowcase or sewing a rectangular-shaped bag from an old sheet. Turn under a 2" hem around the opening and "feed" the piece of rope through it to make a handle, so it can be hung from a hook in the laundry room or a closet. Decorate with permanent markers or tie-dye with some of your homemade dyes. Whenever you need a rag for cleaning paint brushes or polishing the car, dig into the rag bag. It will also provide you with instant resources for craft projects. Need material for a kite tail or a doll dress? You'll be prepared and nothing will go to waste!

INDEX

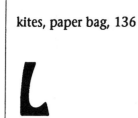

MORE GOOD BOOKS FROM WILLIAMSON BOOKS

Williamson Books are available from your bookseller or directly from Ideals Publications.
Please see last page for contact and ordering information.

Little Hands® Books for Ages 2 to 7:

Parents' Choice Approved
LITTLE HANDS CREATE!
Art & Activities for
Kids Ages 3 to 6
BY MARY DOERFLER DALL

SING! PLAY! CREATE!
Hands-On Learning
for 3- to 7-Year-Olds
BY LISA BOSTON

Parents' Choice Honor Award
KIDS CREATE!
Art & Craft Experiences
for 3- to 9-Year-Olds
BY LAURIE CARLSON

**CREATING CLEVER
CASTLES & CARS**
(From Boxes and Other Stuff)
Kids Ages 3–8 Make Their
Own Pretend Play Spaces
BY MARI RUTZ MITCHELL

KINDERGARTEN SUCCESS
Helping Children Excel
Right from the Start
BY JILL FRANKEL HAUSER

Parents' Choice Recommended
EARLY LEARNING SKILL-BUILDERS
Colors, Shapes,
Numbers & Letters
BY MARY TOMCZYK

American Bookseller Pick of the Lists
MATH PLAY!
80 Ways to Count & Learn
BY DIANE MCGOWAN
& MARK SCHROOTEN

Parents' Choice Gold Award
FUN WITH MY 5 SENSES
Activities to Build
Learning Readiness
BY SARAH. A. WILLIAMSON

SCIENCE PLAY!
Beginning Discoveries
for 2- to 6-Year-Olds
BY JILL FRANKEL HAUSER

Kids Can!® Books for Ages 7 to 14:

MAKING AMAZING ART!
40 Activities Using the
7 Elements of Art Design
BY SANDI HENRY

**THE KIDS'
MULTICULTURAL
ART BOOK**
Art & Craft Experiences
from Around the World
BY ALEXANDRA MICHAELS

American Bookseller Pick of the Lists
Dr. Toy Best Vacation Product
**KIDS' CRAZY ART
CONCOCTIONS**
50 Mysterious Mixtures
for Art & Craft Fun
BY JILL FRANKEL HAUSER

American Bookseller Pick of the Lists
Parents' Choice Recommended
ADVENTURES IN ART
Arts & Crafts Experiences
for 8- to 13-Year-Olds
BY SUSAN MILORD

Parent's Guide Children's Media Award
KIDS' ART WORKS!
Creating with Color,
Design, Texture & More
BY SANDI HENRY

Dr. Toy Best Vacation Product
Parent's Guide Children's Media Award
Learning Magazine Teachers'
Choice Award
CUT-PAPER PLAY
Dazzling Creations from
Construction Paper
BY SANDI HENRY

USING COLOR
IN YOUR ART
Choosing Colors for
Impact & Pizzazz
BY SANDI HENRY

AWESOME OCEAN SCIENCE
Investigating the Secrets
of the Underwater World
BY CINDY A. LITTLEFIELD

SUPER SCIENCE
CONCOCTIONS
50 Mysterious Mixtures
for Fabulous Fun
BY JILL FRANKEL HAUSER

BECOMING THE
BEST YOU CAN BE!
Developing 5 Traits
You Need to Achieve
Your Personal Best
BY JILL FRANKEL HAUSER

Learning Magazine Teachers'
Choice Award
KIDS' EASY-TO-CREATE
WILDLIFE HABITATS
For Small Spaces in City,
Suburb, Countryside
BY EMILY STETSON

Little Hands® and *Kids Can!®* are registered
trademarks of Ideals Publications.